The Benefit of the Doubt
Claiming Faith in an Uncertain World

Frank Clark Spencer

With Sermons by
John B. Rogers, Jr.

Copyright © 2013 Frank Clark Spencer, 22 Degrees Publishing

All rights reserved.

ISBN-10: 0615759475
ISBN-13:978-0615759470

DEDICATION

To my Father and Mother who have passed on faith to me by living with inquisitive minds, loving hearts and helping hands.

CONTENTS

	Acknowledgments	Pg. i
	Introduction	Pg. 3
1	A Question of Doubt	Pg. 9
2	Intellectual Crisis	Pg. 13
3	It's Not About You!	Pg. 21
4	Faith is a Journey	Pg. 29
5	Engaging Heart, Hands and Head	Pg. 35
6	Is God Listening?	Pg. 41
7	Death and Resurrection	Pg. 47
8	Living in Community	Pg. 53
9	Thanks Be to God	Pg. 61
10	Between Faith and Doubt (John Rogers)	Pg. 67
11	Make It as Secure as You Can (John Rogers)	Pg. 75
12	And Some Doubted (John Rogers)	Pg. 85
	Bibliography	Pg. 95

ACKNOWLEDGMENTS

This book would not have been possible without the ministry of my six pastors whose conversations formed the material from which it is drawn.

John B. Rogers, Jr.

Albert G. "Pete" Peery

Jane Summey-Mullinax

Charlie Summers

Rush Otey

Lori Raible

Thank you to Dr. Richard Boyce who served as our moderator. I would also like to thank the supper club members in Charlotte who helped me to hone this material through a series of workshops each Tuesday night in the fall of 2011. Thanks to my readers and editors along the way. Thanks to my children, Aly and Clark who have always pushed me to refine my thinking and whose love inspires me. And most importantly love and thanks to my wife, Melanie, who has always created the room for me to explore. Without her I would not have taken the risk of leaving corporate jobs to pursue the calling that God continues to put in front of me. I have been truly blessed.

The proceeds from this book will go to support

The Montreat Conference Center
and
Union Presbyterian Seminary.

INTRODUCTION

Whenever I am asked to take an oath, or make a public promise, or sign a legal document, I take it very seriously. My wife will tell you that I am probably overboard on that score. I joined a fraternity my freshman year of college. We were of course sworn to secrecy as to the rites of initiation. In the context of the great questions and promises in other walks of life, such a vow given by an 18-year-old to a room full of students seems like a minor event. I acknowledge the truth of that perspective. But, to this day, I have never revealed the secrets entrusted to me. Not to close friends. Not even to my wife. The only other person within my family with whom I will discuss the events of that weekend is my son, because 28 years later, he too took the same vow in the same room. I have made other promises in my life: our wedding vows; partnership agreements; SEC filings; charitable pledges. Some are clearly more important than others, but all demand my fidelity.

I grew up in the Presbyterian Church. I am named for my grandfather, a Presbyterian minister and teacher. I have been an active member of a Presbyterian congregation my whole life. It was natural that I would become involved in leadership. I was first elected a deacon in 1991 and then elder in 1994. In our tradition before officers are installed or ordained, they must answer certain questions about what they believe. Knowing how I feel about fidelity of commitments, you may suspect that I had some significant doubts about how to answer, or even if I could answer the required questions. These questions for ordination to the office of elder are at once simple and exceedingly complex. They embody the deepest questions and conclusions of our Reformed theology. My doubts came to head for me in the process of ordination, but I believe these doubts are the same ones each of us carries into the pew each Sunday. Let us consider the first question of ordination.

> Do you trust in Jesus Christ as your Savior, acknowledge him Lord of all and Head of the Church, and through Him believe in one God, Father, Son and Holy Spirit?

Shouldn't every Christian be able to answer this question with a resounding yes? Maybe so, but the theology inherent runs to very deep issues with which scholars and parishioners have struggled for centuries. What is the nature of a Triune God? Do I believe in God through Jesus, or do I really believe in Jesus as the perfect revelation of God on earth? If Jesus is head of the Church, why is it so fraught with human struggle and disagreement? Do I always trust in Jesus Christ as my Savior or do I waiver? Does the concept of Savior require that I believe the a particular theory of atonement for universal sin? If I am saved from something, what is it I am saved from, Hell? Do I have to believe in Hell? And then the second question,

> Do you accept the Scriptures of the Old and New Testaments to be, by the Holy Spirit, the unique and authoritative witness to Jesus Christ in the Church universal, and God's word to you?

Wow! Now I feel like I am really getting into trouble. There are lots of versions of the Scripture and they each provide a little different point of view. Why don't Protestants include all the books that the Catholics do? Who made that decision? What about the parts I disagree with? What about the parts I just don't like? Who voted on what to put in there anyway? How can we know they are authoritative when scholars in our own denomination can't even agree who wrote the books or even which phrases were part of the original or added later? Are they really unique? Don't other sacred texts reveal truth about God? What about conflicts with science and knowledge? What if I'm not sure about miracles? Weren't things like demonic possession really illnesses that first century writers didn't understand? How can I be sure? If the Bible is literally true, why then are there numerous internal contradictions? But the other view is equally troublesome. If parts of Scripture are to be taken figuratively, then which parts are not? Now then, the third question.

> Do you sincerely receive and adopt the essential tenets of the Reformed faith as expressed in the confessions of our church as authentic and reliable expositions of what Scripture leads us to believe and do, and will you be instructed and led by those confessions as you lead the people of God?

Another 300 pages of footnotes to my oath of office, all explicitly incorporated therein by reference!! What about the disputed version between Presbyterians themselves? Am I claiming the left hand column in the Book of Confessions or the right hand one? This now brings in all the stuff that my modern education has caused me to question. A virgin birth, really? Resurrection? Don't tell me you haven't questioned the literal nature of this claim. In fact, reading the Bible reveals others who were raised from the dead by Jesus and others who also ascended into heaven. What are we to make of all this? What about the second coming? It sure sounds like Jesus meant very soon, not several millennia later.

How could I know? How could I be sure? What could I do in the face of such doubt?

This was not the first time doubt had been a big issue for me. As a 15-year-old, like most 15-year-olds, I had become a professional skeptic. I was questioning anything my parents were teaching and I began to seriously question whether there was value in church beyond the social benefits of youth group and church trips to the mountains. After all, in the mid 1970's everything seemed as if it was up for question. That's when a sermon changed my world view.

In 1975, John Rogers preached a sermon on Faith and Doubt in the Davidson College Presbyterian Church. I was sitting on the left side of the church, a few rows from the back with friends. I didn't sit with my parents when I could avoid it. For whatever reason, that morning I was captivated. That sermon set the direction of my faith development. As I remember, John made several points that struck me then and have stayed with me ever since. First, faith without question, or blind faith, is nothing to which one should aspire. It is dead because it implies no use of one's intellect, no honest examination of one's feelings toward God, no actual engagement of the most critical issues of the soul. However, faith that is affirmed in the face of doubt is more precious than anything. A faith that can question, explore, feel emotion and engage with God is a faith worth having. John gave us permission to bring all questions to God. He assured us that there is no question that we can conceive that will offend or surprise God if those questions come from a sincere desire to understand or stem from a true emotion. The freedom that he gave me on that morning, has allowed me to explore a deepening relationship with God ever since. It has provided the context for my development of a broadly ecumenical religious view and created an appreciation for other traditions even as I embrace my own more deeply.

I was able to answer those questions of ordination affirmatively, not because my doubts were completely dispelled, but rather because I was able to claim my faith in the face of doubt. I can say with the father of the paralytic boy in Mark 9:24, "I believe; help my unbelief."

John Rogers moved on from the church in Davidson and so did I. We have been reunited in Montreat, North Carolina, home to the Montreat Conference Center, a national conference center of the Presbyterian Church (USA). In the intervening 35 years, I have been blessed with pastoral leadership from an extraordinary group of Presbyterian ministers. In December of 2010, six of those pastors came together to examine questions of faith and doubt. They ranged in age from 37 to 70. There are four men and two women. They have led large churches and small churches and new churches. They have traveled the world on mission work and have run countless session meetings in countless church parlors. They have managed budgets, staff and outreach. They have studied, taught and preached. They have celebrated Holy Communion. They have baptized new members, confirmed young adults and laid saints to rest. They have all been my pastor.

Over two days, these six ministers explored intimate views of faith and doubt using sermons by John Rogers as a starting point. Three of those sermons are published here for the first time. A copy of John's 1975 sermon had been miraculously preserved by Rush Otey, the associate pastor in Davidson at the time. I had invited Rush to the conversation before anyone knew he had it. The sermon is reprinted in Chapter 10. Dr. Richard Boyce of Union Presbyterian Seminary served as our moderator, for which we all are deeply grateful.

This subsequent account is written from the point of view of these pastors' common parishioner. In organizing this conversation and publishing the results, I had hoped to accomplish two things. First, I wanted to bring to all who struggle with doubt, the same comfort and freedom I received those many years ago. In reading these pages and discussing doubt with others, I pray that insight develops and that relationships with God are deepened. Second, I hoped to create room for our ordained clergy to express openly the struggles and triumphs that are inherent in all faithful ministry. Too often, we ask our pastors to have all the answers and wisdom and to provide us with comfort. They feel the weight of those expectations. Perhaps our lives in the community of Christ would be enriched if, in having accepted permission to question, we grant our clergy the same permission and thereby let them lead us on a journey that includes the doubt we all experience to a faith that awaits only those who will engage the questions which bother them most.

Those were my original goals in convening this study. The result, as you will see, not only addresses fundamental questions of doubt in its many forms, intellectual, existential, ethical and spiritual, but has broader implications for how we live and worship together in faithful congregations. The discussion did not focus on an argument for the existence of God, but rather examined what the Reformed tradition has to say about how we study, worship and live, embracing a community of faith in the face of doubt. These ministers explored the concepts of constant journey, the sovereignty of God, the faith of the community, death and resurrection, and the Reformed perspective on the good news of the Gospel.

What I thought might be insight into individual manifestations of doubt, instead became a celebration of community faith that may provide insight for our life together as pastors and parishioners.

The process I have followed is not that of a court reporter. There is no attempt to chronicle the conversation and with rare exception, none of the participants is quoted directly. Instead, I have attempted to synthesize the discussion into relevant themes. Each Chapter explores a different aspect of the faith/doubt continuum, and includes questions for reflection and discussion. The sermons in Chapters 10-12 span John Roger's 30 years of distinguished ministry, from the original text in 1975 to a more recent work preached in April of 2004. These sermons provide contemporary insight into age old questions. So, welcome into the discussion. Bring your doubts, your fears, and your questions. They are all welcome here.

1 A QUESTION OF DOUBT

Doubt concerning spiritual and religious matters comes in many forms. Intellectual doubt is a question of synthesizing what we know. It plagues those who struggle with squaring religious doctrine with an understanding of the universe built on scientific discoveries and proofs. Existential doubt finds its home in anxiety and often takes hold when bad things happen and life spins out of control. It is the search for meaning in the events of our lives and the lives of others. Ethical doubt questions how a loving God can allow the evil and suffering we see in the world. Spiritual doubt questions life after death and leads us to wonder about our place in eternity. Doubt does not recognize denomination, faith tradition, time or geography. It is a part of the human condition, but as we will see, so is faith.

We will deal first with doubt that arises when education comes into seeming conflict with the stories of faith as we come to know them in the Scriptures. We will discover that we are often wrong about a good many things and how this affects our perception of doubt. We will explore how apologetics, the defense of the faith, allows us to engage thinking and reason in support of our beliefs. But we will also come to understand that intellect cannot overcome doubt and that doubt is, after all, a part of finite human life.

Contrary to much of popular culture and many current religious voices, we will examine how faith is not a purely individual pursuit. There are two primary external elements of faith, the sovereignty of God and the faith of the community. The sovereignty of God acknowledges that it is God who chooses us and not we who opt for

God. Salvation is a gift we cannot earn no matter how well we behave nor how hard we believe. The apostle Paul says we put on Christ and that we are IN Christ. Theologian Karl Barth says that if we are IN Christ, then so are others also IN Christ and we are thus bound into community. There is no such thing as individual salvation because Jesus did not live and die exclusively for you or for me, but rather for the world. The Church is the single body of Christ. We thus travel a journey together. Even though we are one body, it makes a difference with whom each of us chooses to walk. Doubt is never set aside, but we will find that our fellow travelers may have a deep impact on how our faith is sustained.

If doubt is a constant companion that cannot be overcome by the intellect, how are we to commit to the community of faith. We will explore how complex human beings experience worship, mission, study and prayer with much more than their minds. Heart, hands and head are all engaged in the journey of faith. Faith it turns out is as much about doing as believing.

So what can be the benefit of doubt? We will explore how doubt, and particularly the humility that should accompany it, can bind us into authentic community. Sharing doubts allows us to be vulnerable and connect. It strips away self-importance and judgmental attitudes. It lets us know that others are in the same place of questioning that we are. On the opposite side of doubt is fully engaged worship, penetrating study and fearless action. The ability to doubt becomes a fundamental key to a stable faith. It frees us from a fragile faith that fears engaging the world lest it be shaken.

Doubts about God's action, or perceived inaction have plagued the people of the Bible from the beginning. Will God act on behalf of the covenant community? Does God hear our prayers? What really happens when we die? These are questions that express the doubts of the religious, not the atheist. Doubt, as we are using it here, is not about proving the existence of God. The question of atheism is not one we will address. Our interest here is the struggle that brings faith and doubt into opposition for those who believe in God. Most people on earth and 94% of adults in the United States believe in the existence of God. This book is for them.

The Pew Research Center reports that 75% of US adults self-identify as Christian. My experience is that many of those who self-identify as Christian do not necessarily understand the doctrine of their own tradition and those who do find it difficult to embrace all aspects of that doctrine. Many make little distinction between various Christian denominations and many of the fastest growing churches claim no denominational affiliation at all. The questions I hear coming from adults respect no denominational boundaries but rather focus on the big questions of life and spirituality. The approach to engaging those questions reflected in these pages is by necessity from the Reformed tradition, because all of the pastors who participated in the creation of this work are from that tradition.

The Reformed tradition is the branch of Protestantism that began with John Calvin in Geneva and spread throughout Europe and into the new world. It has since found followers in Asia, particularly in the Korean Presbyterian Church. It spread to the new world predominantly through Scottish, English and Huguenot immigration and is represented today in numerous denominations including The Reformed Church in America, the United Church of Christ, and the Presbyterian Church (USA). The Reformed tradition shares substantial theology with most mainline protestant denominations including the Episcopal, Methodist and Lutheran churches.

Pew Research further reports that 20% of US adults now claim no religious affiliation but only 6% claim no belief in God at all. Further, 14% say they believe in God and are spiritual but not religious. They are called the "nones," as in religious affiliation – none. Something they perceive in contemporary religious practice has pushed them away from the organized church. I suspect it may be a perception that only true believers are welcome. They are caught somewhere between faith and doubt and do not experience the church as a safe place to live out that struggle. This book is an invitation to seek out authentic community within the Reformed tradition.

Frank Clark Spencer

2 INTELLECTUAL CRISIS

"I believe. Help my unbelief!" Mark 9:24

Those of us who were brought up in the Christian tradition, often face the first crisis of faith when the simple faith of childhood crashes headlong into education. For many this occurs during adolescence when the counterweight of scientific, psychological and philosophical inquiry overwhelms religious doctrine. Claims by religious leaders about what seem to be magical events don't square with the rational perspective we are being taught in school. We read about miracles and healing and yet don't see those things in our everyday world. Perhaps miracles are happening around us, but we fail to see them. "How can this stuff be true?" we ask ourselves. Freud tells us belief in God is a collective illusion. Christopher Hitchens goes into great detail to prove that all believers are wrong. Media sensationalists set science against religion to drive viewership or TV ratings. There is nothing like a good controversy to stir things up!

At the other extreme, some never question their faith at all. Those who hold onto faith that cannot be questioned may find that when doubt does indeed break through, they are without the necessary tools to address a world turned upside down. Extreme fundamentalists rely on scriptural inerrancy as the bulwark against doubt. They sport bumper stickers that read, "The Bible says it. I believe it. That settles it." But does it really? The inconsistencies within the Bible itself, the disputes over language and translation, the wildly varying interpretation even between members of the same congregation, all belie a view that the Bible is a single revelation dictated word for word by God. Although it may be divinely inspired, the Bible is better seen as a collection of human writing that points us to the infinite and the saving grace of God in Christ Jesus.

No one can move through this life without discovering that they were wrong about something. Can anyone really be sure they know the absolute truth about God whom our mortal minds cannot comprehend?

In her book, "Being Wrong," Kathryn Schulz takes the reader on funny and disturbing adventures in being wrong about little things and also being wrong on a colossal scale. She explains Carl Jung's paradoxical view that the more adamantly someone defends certain beliefs, the more likely it is that person harbors unspoken doubts and greatly fears admitting those doubts. People who suppress all doubt have less stable belief systems than those who consciously grapple with doubt. For people who embrace ambivalence and co-exist with unresolvable tensions, faith becomes more and more stable. Only the humility to doubt leads to an abiding faith.

If you have picked up this book and have read even these first few pages, it is likely that you have questions, not conclusions. Congratulations! You are on a journey to a deeper faith, for it is only in struggling with your most fundamental doubt that a deeper faith is formed.

The problem is that such a statement is of scant comfort when we are wrestling in a crisis of belief. We carry questions inside us that sometimes bubble up on their own. At other times, conversations with friends, colleagues, or fellow church members raise questions that defy explanation.

> Why does God let bad things happen?

> What is required for my salvation?

> Are faithful people of non-Christian traditions rejected by God and therefore condemned to hell?

Does faith stand in opposition to rationality or scientific principles?

We want someone to give us answers. "Teach me the arguments," we plead. "What can I tell my friends when we get into those discussions of religion and philosophy over dinner or a morning coffee?

What we are asking for is a line of reasoning called apologetics. Despite the negative tone that the word apologetics has for the modern hearer, it does not mean making excuses for but rather provides the rationale for what we believe. Apologetics comes from the Greek word "apologia" and means speaking in defense of. It is the discipline of defending a position or belief using reason and logic. When applied to Christian doctrine, it is the practice of providing rational explanation for belief in God, Christ, salvation and the various theological dogmas of organized Christianity. While some theologians prefer a focus on revelation rather than explanation, in my experience, apologetics is the substance of most conversations about questions of faith and doubt for the average person in the pew. Using one's intellect is how many people engage their faith as they move beyond the adolescent view of truth based on authority, whether adopted from parents or preachers. It is natural that we should apply the skills we learn in school to questions about the nature of the divine and about the church that claims to represent that divine nature on earth.

So apologetics is a place to begin. It allows us to think and reason. It is the door through which we embrace learning and study as a way to better understand our relationship to God. It requires effort, struggle and time. I recall a friend telling about a long car ride home from college with and avowed atheist. Despite hours of testimony and apologetics offered by the believer, the atheist remained unmoved. And so it is with each of us. We cannot hope to find a blinding light of intellectual conversion in a two-hour discussion nor by reading a single treatise on the nature of God. The study that nurtures and sustains one's faith must be ongoing. The greatest theologians of history never got to the end of their work, only to the end of their temporal lives.

In one of the most widely acclaimed books of apologetics "Mere Christianity," C. S. Lewis provides concise arguments for the belief in

God and in Jesus as God incarnate. But he also makes room for those who question and doubt. His views on Christianity and atheism are both amusing and instructive:

> "If you are a Christian you do not have to believe that all the other religions are simply wrong all through. If you are an atheist, you do have to believe that the main point in all the religions in the world is simply one huge mistake. If you are a Christian, you are free to think that all those religions, even the queerest ones, contain at least some hint of truth. When I was an atheist I had to try to persuade myself that most of the human race has always been wrong about the question that mattered to them most; when I became a Christian I was able to take a more liberal view."

What apologetics also affirms is that faith never fears intellectual inquiry. Quite the opposite is true. Dr. Francis Collins, head of the Human Genome Project and Director of the National Institutes of Health, eloquently describes his faith development in his book "The Language of God." Collins' book outlines for us a journey into scientific knowledge that has deepened, not diminished, his faith in a creative God of the universe. Interestingly, both Lewis and Collins were self-avowed atheists as they began their explorations.

Before we go any farther, let me be clear. Faith overcoming doubt is not an exercise of intellect. In fact, one need not adopt a goal for having faith overcome doubt at all. Doubt rides along as the constant companion of faith. Coming to this realization is critical to embracing the faith that you feel in spite of your doubts. Paul Tillich, noted theologian of the mid-20th century has provided insight into the dynamic tension that always exists between faith and doubt. In his book, "Dynamics of Faith," Tillich talks about the finite being who is grasped by and turned to the infinite:

> "Faith is certain insofar as it is an experience of the holy. But faith is uncertain insofar as the infinite to which it is related is received by the finite being. This element of uncertainty in faith cannot be removed, it must be accepted…. To accept this is courage. In the courageous standing of uncertainty, faith shows most visibly its dynamic character."

Debate over the nature of doubt itself highlights the mysterious and uncertain nature of the pursuit we call theology. As Augustine defined it, theology means "reasoning or discussion concerning the Deity." Karl Barth, in his book "Evangelical Theology" offers three aphorisms concerning doubt:

1. "No theologian ... should have any doubt... that he is a doubter."
2. "There is certainly justification for the doubter. But there is no justification for doubt itself (and I wish someone would whisper that in Paul Tillich's ear)."
3. "Doubt indeed has its time and place. In the present period no one, not even the theologian, can escape it. But the theologian should not despair, because this age has a boundary..."

Barth, like Tillich, is telling us that doubt is part of the human condition limited as we are by time, space and imperfect capacity (aphorisms 1 and 3). In aphorism two Barth argues that God, in and of God's self, without any help from us, is certainty, and therefore doubt is ultimately not justified, even in the face of the fact that we mortals cannot escape it. As you can also see from Barth's quote, two of the twentieth centuries most widely read theologians often do not agree. Those of us in the pews can only take this as further confirmation that doubt will not be overcome by intellectual argument.

Thus, we can accept that doubt is a part of the human condition. Embracing that doubt allows us to explore even greater depths of faith. By pressing hard on the issues that leave us disturbed and disquieted, we gain insight. Those who have pursued understanding with the greatest zeal and intellectual discipline are also those who find the greatest wonder and mysteries open up to them. So this intellectual pursuit never threatens faith, but will serve to enhance it.

The passage for this chapter is verse 9:24 in the Gospel according to Mark. It was also the Scripture reading on the day in 1975 that I heard John Rogers' sermon "Between Faith and Doubt," which draws on the apologetic tradition to discuss doubt in ways that resonated with me as I hit my first crisis of intellectual doubt. It provided me with the freedom and courage to follow an uncertain path over 35 years ago. "I believe. Help my Unbelief," is the fulcrum on which the story of Healing the Boy with an Unclean Spirit balances. However, the father's cry for help is not the only point of this very rich passage. In reading not only verses 9:14-29 in Mark, but the passages which precede them, a fuller understanding of the circumstances becomes clear.

This story of healing follows The Transfiguration in all three of the synoptic gospels (Matthew, Mark, Luke). What are we to make of this? Jesus has taken Peter, James and John up to the mountaintop, literally and figuratively. There, Jesus is transformed and Moses and Elijah join him in splendor. Peter is so inspired and yet so focused on the temporal that he suggests building a shrine to preserve the moment. Our inclination to institutionalize the Holy seems hard wired. At that moment, surely the disciples had no doubt about the divine nature of Jesus. God spoke and said, "This is my Son, the Beloved. Listen to him!" All of a sudden, it is only Jesus standing there. The message is clear; Jesus should be the focus of their discipleship, not any other great leader, past, present or future.

Haven't we all wanted that mountaintop moment? Absolute clarity about who is in control? No doubts about to whom we owe allegiance and therewith the courage to actually live it?!

So, what happens? Down off the mountain come the disciples, returning from the realm of spiritual revelation to the mundane of life and work in the valley. Don't we all know that Monday morning feeling, too? As people in the church, we are often inspired at one moment, and then trapped in daily frustration in the next. It doesn't take long for the disciples to encounter a problem they can't solve. Despite their efforts, they can't heal this boy. It seems likely that the argument between the scribes and the disciples stemmed from this failure. Maybe the scribes said, "We told you so. You can't heal just because you follow that preacher from Nazareth." Those words would really sting because the reality was that they hadn't been able to heal the boy. They may have gotten defensive, "Well we know Jesus is the Son of God. We just saw him with Moses and Elijah and you scribes wouldn't question the authority of those two!" Then doubt strikes at the heart of disciples, "If we really know it is true that Jesus is the Son of God, why is the boy still possessed?" I can only imagine Peter,

James and John thinking to themselves, "What is wrong? Why doesn't this work? Are we really sure of that to which we have committed our lives?"

Just then, Jesus shows up. He hears what has been going on and rebukes the disciples, "You faithless generation." For someone who is in the midst of doubting themselves, this is a hard judgment to hear. But there is comfort for us. Jesus is saying "you faithless generation" to Peter and the others, who are the foundation on which the Church will be built. Maybe we can feel better about our own place in the community of followers knowing that even those closest to Jesus struggled with being faithful.

Questions for Study and Reflection

Some readers or classes may want additional discussion of these concepts which can be found in John Rogers' sermons. They are reprinted in Chapters 10-12. For this first chapter, read the sermon, "Between Faith and Doubt," which is an invitation into a journey of faith and doubt. It provided me with the freedom and courage to follow an uncertain path over 35 years ago. I invite you to begin where I did.

1. What things that you hear in church or read in Scripture bother you intellectually?

2. Can you recall a time when your intellectual development challenged your faith?

3. Do you find it harder to share your doubts or your faith with others? Why?

4. Read Mark 9:14-29. Focus on verse 19 and verse 24. What is Jesus saying to his disciples? What is the father saying about his own state of mind? How is this man's statement a potential model for our own prayers?

5. Where in your life have you experienced mystery?

6. John Rogers quotes George Buttrick as saying, " All gratitude is belief." What do you think Buttrick means? How does that phrase relate to faith and doubt as you understand those terms?

3 IT'S NOT ABOUT YOU

"My Lord and My God!" John 20:19

It's not all about you! That phrase may not be the most fashionable in today's world of customized products, online shopping, mommy make-overs and human bodies as walking billboards. We live in a fundamentally self-centered culture. Even old commercial slogans evoke melody and message in the TV generation. I bet you can sing right along with these words:

> "You deserve a break today!"

> or

> "Have it your way!"

From the TV generation to the Facebook generation the self-focus has intensified. We have our own web pages. We tweet about what we are having for lunch, as if anyone really cared. We hire personal college admissions coaches, personal trainers, personal shoppers, financial planners, lawyers, and accountants, all to improve the life of ME Incorporated.

But it's not all about ME, at least not when we talk about faith. There are two dimensions of this external dynamic to which we should pay particular attention. The first is that God is sovereign. God has set forth the plan for the world. We know God through God's revelation to us. The fact of God's sovereignty has definite implications for the question of faith.

Within the Reformed tradition, we believe that everything in the universe and every life lived in the universe belongs to God. The response of the creature (you and me) is not essential to that creature's belonging to God. It may be very important to that creature's living in the knowledge that he or she belongs to God, and the richness of life that flows from that knowledge, but even in the absence of a response on the part of the creature, the deepest truth about that life is that life belongs to God and God will not let it go. Said more simply, God exists and has dominion over the universe whether you choose to believe it or not. It is basic to our Reformed tradition that we acknowledge that we don't choose God. God chooses us.

There is a presumption at the core of our theology that one is most faithful and fulfilled when one accepts the grace of God. That grace is God's intention for you. That is who you are. The community of faith proclaims this fact whether you believe it or not. There is no place you can run from God's Spirit. God is never going to give up on you. When you live into that reality is when you are going to be more fully who God intends you to be. This attitude leads to a grateful life, not a life that has to prove its own worthiness over and over to be accepted.

We best understand how God's sovereignty intersects with our lives when we see that God has a purpose and intention for our lives, rather than a plan. That purpose has to be something each of us has a hand in shaping so that it draws out our talents. If we are living with a sense of purpose, with an undergirding that God has an intention for each of us, that understanding is comforting and liberating. It is also challenging. We can't take the comfort and just do as we please. We have to give prayerful and thoughtful consideration to how we want to live accepting of the knowledge that we belong to God. Such is the essence of faith.

If we belong to God, then we should seek to know God and know about God. But how do we know God? Nature testifies to God as creator. Scripture guides us and tells the story of God's relationship with humankind. But it is in the person of Jesus Christ that we see the supreme revelation. In Jesus Christ we have to deal with God's very self and not just someone who is like God. This was the issue of debate at the Council of Nicea, the divinity of Christ Jesus. When we acknowledge that God is sovereign, the affirmation of God incarnate that has occurred in the birth, life, death and resurrection of Jesus Christ has implications for the whole universe. However, to acknowledge the truth of that claim requires the ceding of control by the individual because our finite minds cannot fully grasp the concept of an infinite God engaging humankind in this way. Ceding control is something most of us fear on many levels. The first fear is the ceding of intellectual control. One minister tells of his struggle in college,

> "I thought I was in control of my mind. My crisis was the question of surrendering my mind and my doubts to religion or trusting the order that I was discovering through science and mathematics."

The second fear is subjugating the egocentric self to an outside power. Some people live with the myth that they are in control of their lives and like the idea that the church reinforces order rather than challenges order. For the most part, they want the church to fit as an aspect of control in their lives, helping raise children in a moral way. They believe that if they are respectful to God and God is therefore respectful to them, everything will be neat and orderly. Then something major comes along, the death of spouse or a child with a debilitating illness, and that sense of order is shattered. They can often spin out of control and be plunged into the existential questions of the psalmist.

In the case of our intellectual friend, the church can be off putting when creeds and dogma take too prominent a role. For our beleaguered spouse or parent, those same creeds and dogma become a source of comfort, reassurance and certainty in a time of turbulence. How can the church possibly meet the opposite needs of these two?

The answer lies in the faith of the community. This is the second external element of faith. Faith exists within a community rather than as the province of one soul, one mind or one heart. The faith of a community takes on dimensions that eclipse the capacity of any individual. The first time I heard this concept, I wasn't sure what exactly to make of it. How can a community have a faith? Surely faith is something we must each wrestle with for ourselves. Like Jacob, I will grapple all night and will not let go of God until I am victorious or vanquished. But it is my individual struggle. Ironically, that attitude captures both the intellectual and the egotist in all of us.

But it's not about me. It's about God and God's faith in God's people, us. It is the community that preserves and passes the faith down to the next generation. The community is there for me when I need support and sometimes I am there when others need help. Even sinners and doubters can bear witness to the sovereignty of God and to God's faithfulness to us. In this sense the faith of the church relieves me of having to have it all sorted out myself. I become part of the community that has wrestled with these same issues for centuries, and is still wrestling because we are not finished and will never be finished. The same minister who suffered the crisis of doubt in college now has a different view,

> "That's where I was but I now have discovered that the church, and specifically the Presbyterian Church (USA), is a place that it is OK to keep that struggle going."

Creeds and confessions help us sort out some of these things. They represent the collective wisdom of the faith community at different times and under different circumstances. Some are used more often than others, but they are not a litmus test for belonging. Underlying our understanding of what the faith community proclaims are the creeds of the church. Not our individual creeds, and if I feel I can't say one at any given time, the church is going to say it anyway. We don't have to be literalistic about a creed any more than we have to be literalistic about Scripture. Without demanding of yourself an absolute standard, you can take your stand among the community that says these things. Let the community help you move in your own pilgrimage along with them until you can say your own creed.

This is indeed a very different concept from what we are confronted with today, living in a sea of volunteeristic faith where people ask, "If you died tonight, do you know that you would be going to heaven?" The unspoken counterpart is the threat that if you answer wrongly, you will be going to hell. In other words, the choice is up to you, intellectually, emotionally, and spiritually. What a lonely and scary place for everyone who has doubt (everyone) to stand. Those with such fears are likely to cover them up, push them aside and keep such thoughts secret. This only serves to isolate people and shuts down the opportunity for conversation and growth.

There are lots of people who are "covering their bets," dealing with doubt using the following calculus, "If Jesus Christ is the only way to heaven, I better profess him as Lord and get my ticket punched, and if he's not, then I haven't lost anything." Do we really believe that the essence of what God did for us in Jesus Christ is simply to increase our options? Or did God give us life to live today and life eternal? If it is the former, that puts God in the role of a used car salesman saying, "I've got a deal for you but it is going away if you don't take it."

Worse still, that puts the individual in control of one's own salvation, a very selfish and egocentric view. In fact, holding self as central can be the source of profound doubt. We all have limited capacity and will inevitably fail when we rely solely on our own intellect, spirituality or discernment. So instead of the self-centered view enhancing a sense of personal power, the result is a feeling of powerlessness. Others then exploit the fearful and disillusioned as we have seen in many of the notorious cases of churches breaking the trust of the community.

Our Reformed theology specifically rejects the idea that each individual controls his or her fate relative to personal salvation. In fact, it is not only OK to die with doubt; it is inevitable that each of us will. God has acted in the birth, life, death and resurrection of Jesus Christ and through that grace has redeemed the world. Our human response is not determinative of the mind of God.

Thus, the community of faith that proclaims the truth of God's revelation in Christ Jesus and welcomes those who doubt, wherever they are in their journey, is the place where faith can build and develop in safety.

"Wherever you are, there we will meet you."

That should be our communal promise. This is not to say that whatever an individual believes is right and true and that's OK. Such an attitude breeds a consumption notion of the church, a desire to extract whatever good I can for myself and move on. Faith builds over time as one lives, studies and worships in a community. That is how we live Anselm's credo of faith seeking understanding.

In John's gospel Chapter 20 verses 24-29, we encounter the Bible's most famous doubter, Thomas. Recall Thomas was not present at the risen Jesus' first appearance to the disciples. He would like to believe but he is of a skeptical nature. After all, the story that the others have told him is quite fantastical. Christ says to Thomas, "Put your finger here and see my hands. Reach out your hand and put it in my side. Do not doubt, but believe." Thomas answered him, "My Lord and my God!" This response has been described as worship.

Describing those words as worship is correct, but Thomas's response is also creedal in nature. As we dissect Thomas's short creed, two important elements emerge. The first is the acknowledgement of Jesus as Lord. In other words, Thomas is swearing allegiance to Jesus as the leader, "My Lord." He is pledging loyalty to Jesus personally and to the community he is leading. The second part of the creed is a declaration of faith in Christ as sovereign ruler of the universe, "My God." This second declaration of faith is much more radical than the promise of loyalty. In fact, this is the first time in Scripture that Jesus is referred to as God, and not one of the subordinate titles of Son of God, Son of Man, or even Messiah.

In the church today, it seems that many of us may find ourselves suspended between the two halves of Thomas's creed. This derives from the centrality of the risen Jesus in the Church. It is the Word made flesh and God's subsequent demonstration of power over death that causes all of the doubts we have discussed thus far to come crashing in. It brings intellectual doubt back into play.

Did God really suspend natural laws in this way and others throughout Jesus' ministry? But the resurrection also brings the existential doubt into play. Did God choose to act in this way on behalf of the community, a community expanded to now include all of humankind?

If God has thus acted, this would fulfill the promise to Abraham that "in you all the families of the earth shall be blessed" (Gen 12:3). On the other hand, the second half of that claim is certainly new territory for the disciples who view God and Jesus in the context of the chosen people of Israel. So we see that doubt is present even at the heart of our good news; that God through Christ Jesus has acted for all time to claim the lives we live in this world. Maybe you can say Jesus is Lord. By that you mean that you take your stand in the community that claims Jesus Christ as head of the Church. Maybe you can't yet profess Jesus as God incarnate. The community can. There is room for you in the community of faith wherever you fall along the spectrum. The journey, if you are willing to make it, will eventually bring you to doubting your doubts.

Questions for Study and Reflection

1. Read John 20:24-29. Do you find skeptics like Thomas reassuring or disturbing? How would you describe yourself?

2. How does the faith of the community manifest itself in your congregation?

3. Have there been times when the faith of others has sustained your own faith?

4. How does the claim that God is sovereign shape the way we think about events in the world?

5. Is it comforting or disturbing to realize that your salvation is not dependent on your choices?

6. At different times, do you feel yourself at different places along Thomas' spectrum of belief?

7. From your perspective, does the church do more to reinforce order or to challenge order? How do you feel about that?

4 FAITH IS A JOURNEY

"It Overcame his Fear," <u>The Lord of the Rings</u>, JRR Tolkien

While each individual experiences the journey of faith differently, there are often similarities even if we begin the stages at very different ages of life.

When I was growing up in the South of the 1960's and 70's, it was still presumed that you went to church because your parents did. Although the generational breakdown of institutions that would continue to grow in America through the close of the 20th century had already begun, my experience was not significantly different from the generation that preceded me. For those who grow up in a religious community, there is an assumption of faith. Whether through Presbyterian confirmation, baptism in the Southern Baptist tradition or a Bar Mitzvah, the young adult is expected to take his or her place among the people of faith through a public profession. These ceremonies usually take place at age 12 or 13 for both boys and girls.

A few defiant teenagers resist, but most do not, having come to see the community of faith as a part of their lives. For many, this stage of faith can be described as an emotional, adolescent faith. We didn't want to disappoint parents or be left out of our peer group. After all, by this point we had heard the stories of our tradition and they were comforting and magical. It felt right to believe in the adults' religion now that we were enough years past Santa and the Tooth Fairy to shake off the disappointment when our faith first had been shattered.

I was the youngest of four children, six years younger than my closest sibling. With an obvious eye to self-interest, my brother and sisters guarded the Santa myth with great care and expert execution. As the reality began to dawn on me before my eighth Christmas, I found myself doubting my doubts. I remember going to my 13-year-old sister and wanting to make sure I had my bases covered I said, "I believe in Santa but I think it might be Mom and Dad who get the presents. If you find out for sure, promise you'll tell me so that I won't disappoint my children."

My intellect had pierced a set of important beliefs, beliefs that were tied up in morality, generosity, and love. In my experience, the same thing will happen to most of those who make the religious public profession at the start of adolescence. For some, that inevitable intellectual doubt will cause a tearing of the fabric of faith. Many leave the church at that point, aided by the physical removal from home associated with college, military service or a first job and apartment. Others push doubt away. They seek the comfort of certainty in an uncertain adolescent world. We should mourn for them because it is likely that when doubt comes, if not through intellectual concern then when life seemingly falls apart, the crash is often extreme. They can't fathom how they got where they are. It is they who need the care and support of other believers most urgently.

Others find that intellectual pursuit changes the way they view faith without shaking it. They are fired by loving God with their minds and not just their hearts. Ultimately, the quest for knowledge in the context of faith opens them to greater energy and mystery. Such people are important teachers and guides for us. They have not shunned the mind, but rather have found that by allowing faith to engage intellect, they have come to deeper, simpler truths. The cycle looks something like this although it is not always linear:

Initial faith;

Doubt or disappointment;

Examination;

Understanding;

Deeper faith;

This pattern begins not only in adolescence, but at whatever point one acknowledges the reality of God and joins a tradition of those who seek to know and understand that reality. The human condition is such that this is not a one-time process, but one that will repeat itself over and over and over again.

Today, many people are not raised in a stable faith community. The concept of community expectation around faith development may not exist at all. Or, what may have gotten through are the louder, TV oriented manifestations of Christianity that condemn, shout, and threaten. Many of our brothers and sisters sitting in the pews with us may have come to the church only recently or have returned after many years. They may be there for child rearing purposes, a frequent motivation for young adults. For whatever reason, they have joined the faith community, the band of travelers.

Perhaps because JRR Tolkien was a friend and confidant of C.S. Lewis, perhaps because I have now reached the age at which first Bilbo and then Frodo set out upon their adventures, perhaps because the tale of courage, doubt, betrayal and redemption resonates with all of us, or perhaps because I have always loved the story itself and the characters who inhabit Middle Earth, my thoughts are drawn back to <u>The Lord of the Rings</u> when I think about faith and how it develops over time.

> "...his [Frodo's] fiftieth birthday drawing near.... at that age that adventure had befallen Bilbo. Frodo began to feel restless and the old paths seemed too well-trodden. He looked at maps and wondered what lay beyond their edges.... He took to wandering further afield and more often by himself.... his { } friends watched him anxiously....' I have sometimes thought of going away.... and I suppose I must go alone if I am to do that and save the Shire. But I feel small and very uprooted and well – desperate... but as he was speaking a great desire to follow .... flamed up in his heart.... It was so strong that it overcame

his fear: he could almost have run out there and then….' "And Gandalf advises, "But I don't think you need to go alone. Not if you know anyone you can trust, and who would be willing to go by your side – and that you would be willing to take into unknown perils. But if you look for a companion, be careful in choosing."

There it is, a full blown mid-life crisis: a crisis of intellect; a crisis of vocation; a crisis of meaning; a crisis of relationship. Translated into our modern vernacular Frodo seems to be asking, "Is this all there is to life? How should I spend my time? Is there anyone who really understands what I am going through? Is this something I've got to do? Can I make a difference for my community?" What this passage shows, and what so many of us live out, is that the crisis of faith is not exclusive to the young. Doubt always reserves the right to raise its head at any point and stop us dead in our tracks. But therein lies the mysterious gift of cognitive power that, as Tillich points out, ever mixes the certainty of the Holy with the inability of the finite being to ever exist in certitude.

Doubt for Frodo, like doubt in our own lives compels and propels us to new discovery of ourselves, our relationships, the world and the nature of God. It is through restlessness that Frodo begins exploration, to venture beyond the edges of the map. It is through the resulting journey that he, his friends, and his world is changed. In <u>The Lord of the Rings</u>, Tolkien has given us an allegory for the nature of God. The fate of the world is put in the hands of an unlikely and reluctant hero, something we see time and again in Scripture. Think of the aged Abraham and Sarah, the stuttering Moses, the inexperienced David, the teenage Mary, the uneducated Peter. They are, like Frodo, ones who should not be able to succeed based on the accepted norms of the world in which they live. Despite feelings of selfishness and ultimately a rejection of the task itself by Frodo, the ring bearer, the task is nonetheless accomplished and the world is redeemed. The outcome for which the journey began is achieved in spite of, rather than because of, the hero.

As modern Christian travelers, we find that we will be confronted with adventures of our own. They are unlikely to include creatures from Middle Earth, but our adventures often hold danger, evil and pain. They also hold opportunity, goodness and joy. How we navigate the landscape of modern life will be dramatically affected by our company of travelers. The people with whom we associate and from whom we draw our values will shape the way we respond to the challenges and opportunities we encounter. Our traveling companions can help sustain our faith even as our doubts propel us to journey on.

What does the concept of journey say to us as we move through the world with our constant companions of faith on the one hand and doubt on the other? First, listen to your doubts. Accept the questions that dog you. Embrace them and examine them, for that very process will lead you to greater understanding. Like Frodo, allow yourself to wonder what is beyond the edge of the map. Venture further afield.

Second, don't allow doubt to stop you. Doubt raises questions. Faith is the courage to act. Had Tolkien left Frodo in Bag End pondering the mysteries of life, it would have been a boring story indeed, albeit much shorter. It is the journey itself of which life is made. Those who seek only "a plot of land and peace and quiet" miss out on the fabulous adventure that the journey provides. We see this emphasis on movement and action with Jesus. Jesus's great commission was not to sit at home and contemplate your God, but "go therefore and make disciples of all nations, baptizing them in the name of the Father, the Son and the Holy Spirit and teaching them to obey all that I have commanded you." Matthew 28: 19-20

Third, listen to the good advice that Gandalf gave to Frodo. Pick those with whom you travel wisely. Those with whom you journey become the critical part of the journey itself. Had Tolkien merely described the terrain which Frodo covered, the work might be hailed as an achievement of descriptive fantasy writing, but it would not hold our interest. It is Frodo's traveling companions, the Elves, the Dwarfs, the Ents, Gandalf and the Hobbits who pull us in. So it is in our own lives. When we surround ourselves with people whom we can trust, who will walk by our side, even into unknown peril, we have chosen wisely. This has been true in my own faith journey. I find myself sustained by spending time with those in whom I have seen God's transforming action. My faith is strengthened by the very faith that I see in others.

Think about times when you have found the most fun, the most meaning and the greatest satisfaction in life. It is always with others, never as a solitary pursuit. The greatest mountain treks have never been accomplished alone. For the golfers among us, would you rather hit that hole-in-one alone on the course, or with three of your best friends looking on and celebrating with you? What makes a baptism, wedding or funeral meaningful is the gathering of loved ones. It is the travelers more than the terrain that makes the journey meaningful.

Questions for Study and Reflection

1. When has doubting something led you to a new discovery or a new insight?

2. Think about a time you took a road trip with friends or family. What made it fun or exciting?

3. For you, where are the edges of the map that you would like to explore?

4. Who has been an important person for you in your faith journey?

5. Read Psalm 73. How does "going into the sanctuary of God" help you in your faith journey?

6. Read Matthew 28:16-20. What do these verses say to us about how we are to live our lives in the face of doubt?

5 ENGAGING HEART, HANDS AND HEAD

"'You shall love the Lord your God with all your heart, and with all your soul, and with all your mind,' This is the greatest and first commandment." Matthew 22:37-38

Some have left the church because they can't deal with what they call "the Jesus myth," often because of intellectual conflict they see between the laws of nature and the claims of Scripture. In my experience, few claim to be atheists. Many, in fact, return with families at holidays or funerals and take joy or comfort in the rhythm, music and familiarity of worship. They set aside their intellectual criticism in the spirit of love and relationship. Therein lies a clue to understanding faith as a realm that exists beyond the arguments of logic, philosophy and pure intellect.

It is clear to those who participate, that worship is more than cognitive. It is the whole person who engages in worship. God has created us as complex beings, with intelligence, emotion, sensation and perception. Consequently, no aspect of worship should be emphasized at the expense of the others. Worship, as an expression of our love for God, must be broadly experiential even as it engages our minds. Different aspects of worship reach us on different planes. In each element of the worship experience, we must keep the countervailing forces in mind. We need to be attentive to theological underpinnings of our worship at the same time we embrace feeling and experience in our hymnody, in our sermons, and in our prayers. In this context, the sermon is different from a theological treatise or lecture, in that it must reach beyond an intellectual argument. It is indeed proclamation. When it comes to creedal affirmations, in a sense theology is the first cousin of poetry and it may be that the deepest convictions are better sung than said.

There is substantial risk to the life of the congregation when one element of worship becomes overemphasized. In the past, the mainline protestant churches may have been too focused on head and where for some, the intellectual argument for faith was lost, so were lost the members of congregations. By contrast, other congregations may be risking running the other way by going with what just feels good. In this we may be selling our own parishioners short.

The growth in non-denominational churches may be driven by short term comfort when one is told what to believe and what to do. If you are strung out, a simple, directive message may provide real comfort. You simply don't have to work very hard at faith. Parishioners get "Jesus loves them" but that is unlikely to sustain them over time. Many of our younger members who have found their way back to mainline churches are recovering from the disappointment inherent in that kind of easy salvation. Our Reformed congregations need to be an oasis for people who want to love God with their minds as well as their hearts. So how should we consider the doubt, and the doubters, that are always a part of worship?

Worship is an essential part of the corporate life of a community of faith. It has always been so. In fact, worship could be said to be the counterpoint to doubt. In Christ's temptation, the promise of kingdoms is based on bowing and worshipping Satan. Jesus quotes Deuteronomy by saying, "Worship the Lord your God and serve God alone." In the context of the early church, worship was a political statement because Caesar demanded worship from his subjects. Worship is moving in a different direction from doubt. Worship is about choosing before whom you bow down. Who or what do you acknowledge as sovereign? The choices are endless: the market; the government; I myself; my family; my talents; God. So while our personal conclusions about faith and doubt are not, and cannot be, determinative of the mind of God, who or what we choose to worship is indeed up to us.

In worship, the community of faith invites the doubter in each of us to participate fully. At the same time, the liturgy itself is trying to call us out of hesitation (hesitation is the Greek word for doubt) and get us moving again in a faithful direction. Just as courage is not the absence of fear but rather action in spite of fear, so is faith action (worship, study, and mission) in the face of doubt.

While worship must engage all aspects of our complex humanity, worship alone is not sufficient for the community of faith nor for its individual members. The greatest commandment does not refer only to worship. In fact, if that were so, we would be a hollow community indeed. No, we are called to engage the whole of creation with the whole of ourselves: heart; hands; head.

When Christ teaches us that in the face of each neighbor, there he is, we are expected to engage each other on a personal level. When this happens, we experience so much more than intellectual understanding of social justice, as important as that may be. We experience the humanity of others in all its variations, joyful and dejected, powerful and helpless, wise and foolish, evil and loving. We cannot help but be affected by the relationships that are formed, whether those relationships last years, days or only minutes.

Within the community of faith, when we see that someone is struggling with doubt, one valid response may be to encourage that person to share in ministry, rather than offering theological arguments for the sovereignty of God or for the atonement of sin in Christ's death on the cross. Often, we need to practice following Christ in the world more than we need further education. We must love God with all of our heart, soul and mind. In fact, with Jesus, there is always a bias for action. He doesn't say sit still and worship, he tells us to move to the next step. It is the same way with a healthy faith community that says, "Come on along. We are moving forward and your doubts won't keep you from coming with us."

This is not to deny the intellect in any way. In fact, once we can embrace our own emotional and spiritual complexity, the study of Scripture and theology does nothing but deepen the experience of worship and mission. Understanding that the order of worship has theological significance makes it more meaningful. Why do we say a corporate prayer of confession when other traditions have nothing similar? Why do the prayers of the people follow the proclaiming of the Word? Why do we use the phrase, "Following the Word into the World?"

Our music is rich with inspiration and helps us to understand our relationship with God and humanity. Many times, we feel emotions triggered by singing familiar hymns. Often those emotions were not consciously accessible but come flooding in to remind us of loved ones gone or events that have shaped our lives. I cannot sing the hymn that was sung when I was ordained as an elder without the same sense of call, joyful and terrifying, returning with equal poignancy.

The life of faith requires that we engage heart, hands and head, that is to say worship, mission and study. One aspect absent the other two loses its impact. Just as one strand of fiber within a rope by itself may be insufficient to carry a load, the intertwined same fibers are more than sufficient. We can claim each of these when we take our place in a faith community because the community is always working on all three aspects of faith in one form or another. What follows is an expression of how doubt evolves and faith is sustained through changing emphasis for a deeply committed Christian. A close friend shared with me his changing perspectives:

> "There have been times for me when loving others seemed to be the anchor of my faith. The whole thing about God as my protector and the one who keeps me safe just didn't seem to be true for me or for most other people. So there was a time that I had doubt about God, but a love for Jesus and I felt Jesus loved me.
>
> There have also been times when I think the whole incarnation, death and resurrection may be a fantasy, albeit a nice one that helps me survive. But the ultimate thing is God, a creator. We need to reclaim the first two chapters of Genesis and the last two chapters of Revelation. Too often the Church focuses on everything between Genesis 3 [The Fall] and Revelation 20 [The Brimstone]. We need to reclaim the creation and the new creation.

In a sense that is a theocentric view, but I have come to believe that none of it makes sense, historically or theologically, without the God/Christ connection."

This insight into one person's sustaining faith, despite the ups and downs of doubt, is a beautiful illustration of how we need different types of engagement at different times in our lives. Sometimes it is enough to be with others in the community and experience love, receiving meals in a time of family distress or giving of oneself in outreach mission. At other times, our intellect and spirit marvel at the grandeur of God and we are inspired to study, teach or worship. Recognizing that we all will experience ups and downs, our ability to take our stand within the community of faith is dependent on engaging with our heart, our soul and our mind.

The Gospel according to Matthew ends with a brief account of the risen Jesus commissioning the disciples on the mountain in Galilee. We are told "When they saw him, they worshipped him; but some doubted." Then Jesus gave them all the instructions to "go therefore and make disciples of all nations, baptizing them in the name of the Father, the Son and Holy Spirit." It is not just the ones who believe absolutely who are commissioned. There is no creedal affirmation required for service. There is only making one's stand as a member of the community that is required. God will do the rest. It is in grateful obedience that the disciples venture forth as a part of a community dependent on the Holy Spirit to be the body of Christ in the world.

Questions for Study and Reflection

"But Some Doubted," in Chapter 12, celebrates community and worship that not only allows the doubters to participate, but welcomes them in. As you read this sermon, reflect on how including those who may not be sure can be an act of hospitality.

1. Read Matthew 22:34-39. How does your congregation engage heart, soul, and mind?

2. Reread Matthew 28:16-20. How does Jesus' commission tie into what he told us earlier in Matthew 22?

3. Describe a time when one aspect of faith was stronger than others for you?

4. How has your view of faith and God evolved over time?

5. Do you have friends or family members who have left the Church? What led to their decisions?

6. Can you think of examples that would support the contention, "It is often easier to act yourself into a new way of thinking than to think yourself into a new way of acting?"

6 IS GOD LISTENING?

"How long, O Lord?" Psalm 13:1

In the second chapter, we dealt with doubt in the form of questioning veracity. That is what atheism is at its heart, a disputation of the claim that God exists. It is the argument that Christopher Hitchens makes in his book, "God is Not Great." He has rationally decided that God is a Freudian illusion that we create in order to survive and make ourselves feel more comfortable. This is a very modern concern.

The father of the possessed boy in Mark 19-24 surely believes that God exists, however, it is apparent that he has some questions about who Jesus is and whether Jesus has the power to heal. This is an aspect of intellectual doubt because the father is unsure about the claims he has heard about Jesus. This is only one of many examples of intellectual doubt that crop up in Scripture. This kind of doubt asks questions about how or why things have happened. Much of the Old Testament is an exercise in trying to understand what has occurred. Think about the Israelites enslavement in Egypt, their subsequent liberation, the realization of the promised land only to lose it again in exile.

In contrast, the Bible does not have expressions of doubt as to God's existence. The basis of the Scripture is an acknowledgement of God, and is an account of our relationship with God. What we find in biblical doubt is a questioning of the nature of God's relationship to us. Will God act? Will God be faithful to God's promises? Will God be just? Has God abandoned us? Those are biblical concerns and have always been a part of the life of the faithful. We find this kind of existential doubt throughout the Psalms.

The Psalms speak to the human condition in unique and beautiful ways. They give voice to the dark night of the soul. We know God is there, but how can God seem so distant? We question evil in the world, and surely there are evil things. We call God's justice into question as we see some who prosper while disregarding all that Scripture teaches us about love and forgiveness. Misfortune befalls those who live lives of faith and compassion.

Psalm 13 is brief, but lays out the doubt and trust of the faithful. "How long, O Lord? Will you forget me forever?" the psalmist asks. To whom is he speaking? To God of course. He never doubts the existence of the Almighty and pleads for God to be present in his life. "Consider and answer me, O Lord my God!" This is indeed personal. It is "my God" to whom the psalmist appeals. He is asking for direct and personal consideration. "But I trusted in your steadfast love." This is the conclusion of faith over and against the anguish of doubt and sorrow. The psalmist proclaims for all of us that even though we suffer in our present circumstances, we proclaim the majesty and justice of the God of all creation.

Psalm 13 follows the pattern of most of the psalms of lament. That pattern has a cry to God. A complaint if you will. The lament expresses doubt that God will provide those things which we expect and want from our God. Following a pause, the psalmist returns to praise and recognition that God is indeed in charge and that God's majesty and sovereignty must be proclaimed. Even Psalm 22 (that Jesus prayed on the cross), "My God, my God, why hast thou forsaken me?" moves eventually to "for dominion belongs to the Lord."

In fact, the pattern holds for all the Psalms except for one, Psalm 88. Psalm 88 is the doubter's anthem. It expresses the depths of despair with no end. The pause, in which we wait for the concluding praise of God's infinite rule, lasts for hundreds of years. There is no reassurance that God will act ever again. This psalm leaves us hanging on the wrong side of doubt. Yet even here, the psalmist concedes that

God is "God of my salvation." The psalmist, in the deepest fear, looks not to self-help for salvation but has an abiding faith in God's ultimate control. He asks hopefully if God's reign extends beyond this life into the next. He is near death and perhaps he seeks the relief that death may bring from the terrors of this life. Perhaps death is indeed the pause without end, the ultimate question that we all must face.

The psalms are songs that serve as prayers to a personal God. But what if we presume this personal relationship, and nothing happens? In fact, I suspect most of us feel like the author of Psalm 88, in that prayers often seem to go unanswered. We wonder if they are also unheard. Either conclusion leaves us unsettled. Why do we keep praying? For those who have experienced answers to prayer, the reasons are obvious. For those who have not, sometimes a story about someone who has experienced an answer to prayer is enough to inspire hope.

Rev. Ted Wardlaw, President of Austin Seminary tells the story of a staff member in the Intensive Care Unit of a local hospital.

> One night, at the end of a long day, one of Central Presbyterian's beloved staff members, a man named Lynn, went home and, since there was still daylight, decided to take his dog for a walk. They walked along the edge of a city park in his Southwest Atlanta neighborhood, and, while they were walking, Lynn was attacked, robbed, stabbed in the heart and left for dead. The dog ran away but, because the dog was on a leash, eventually others noticed his incessant barking and followed him to where Lynn lay unconscious and bleeding heavily. EMS personnel were called and they got Lynn to Grady Hospital's Emergency Room, where doctors performed restorative heart surgery but were not at all optimistic that he would make it through the night.
>
> The next day, I assembled a great measure of Central's staff in the Chapel, where we conducted a prayer service for Lynn. Scripture was read and then, during our prayer time, the staff – some thirty or so assembled – made a circle around the communion table and held hands. I prayed the sort of prayer I often pray when one's recovery seems hopeless, a wimpy little

prayer of resignation – "Lord, when we cannot change the tragedy of a situation, then change us, we pray, in order to accept your will beyond our capacity to even fathom what it is…" – it was a dainty little prayer like that. Other people prayed, too, and then, it was Clarence's turn to complete the prayer. His prayers were always welcomed and appreciated by everyone on that staff, because to experience them was to sense that Clarence and God were on a first-name basis. And, as usual, this particular prayer did not disappoint.

Clarence thanked God for the day before us, for the gift in life, and especially for the gift of Lynn's life (in that sense, his prayer resembled mine – up to this point). But then he took an argumentative tone with God, as if he were grabbing God by the lapel collars and wrestling God to the ground. His voice rose in pitch: "Now, Lord, you know you've done the impossible before! You did it with the Israelites leaving Egypt! You did it with them again when they were wandering in the wilderness! Lord, over and over again, you KNOW you've made a way out of a no way … and you've done it with me, too, Lord. You know it!! And you can do it again, Lord." Now his voice was screeching: "Ple-e-ease, Je-e-e-e-sus! Please! You KNOW you can do it again."

When Clarence's prayer was over, we stood there, silent, some of us weeping, in that circle. Gradually, we composed ourselves and prepared to leave the chapel. But in my heart, I knew that Lynn was going to be all right. How would God dare not answer the fervent prayer of that holy man, Clarence, with whom God was on such good speaking terms? I left that chapel knowing that Lynn would live. And he did. It took months for him to be dismissed from I.C.U., but he lived. He recovered. And Clarence taught me something important about prayer.

Was Lynn's recovery an answer to prayer? You would have a hard time convincing any within the circle that it was not.

When I was working in real estate, I had occasion to walk a wooded lot that was under consideration for development of an apartment complex. In making my inspection, I came across a homeless man who had constructed an elaborate camp. I had no intention of chasing him off. With what I intended as kindness I warned him that there would be a number of people coming to the site over the next few weeks and that he should be on his guard. That night, working on my Sunday school lesson on the parable of Lazarus and the rich man (Luke 16:19-31), it became clear to me that I had met Lazarus earlier in the day. I prayed for guidance and courage. I decided to go back and engage "Lazarus." As we sat and ate the picnic lunch I had brought along, he said to me, "I've been praying for God to send someone to find me." He had come to the United States as a student at a college where his uncle was on the faculty. When his scholarship ran out, he took a job to keep going but lost that in the recession. He became homeless. After I had visited a few more times, he admitted that he was living in sight of his uncle's house but that he was too ashamed to go home. Over the next month, I built trust with this man and established contact with his uncle. That encounter led to a reconciliation with his family, ending more than a year of homelessness for him. Whose prayers were answered? Undoubtedly, both of ours were.

This longing for comfort and the doubt that God is engaged with us in our tribulations is not just an Old Testament problem; it is, like intellectual doubt, a part of the human condition. In her letters from Calcutta, Mother Teresa, that paragon of Christian compassion, reveals deep anguish in her wrestling with her own doubt. But Mother Teresa kept moving forward, kept living as though she were sure, kept following the loving example of Christ despite her doubts and fears. This ability to move forward is critical to claiming the life of faith in the face of our doubts. Sometimes we have to act as if something is true, in order to keep going, and eventually our faith will catch up.

In the birth, life, death and resurrection of Jesus Christ, we Christians believe that circumstances have been transformed from those described in Psalm 88. When we wonder, with the psalmist, if God's salvation will extend beyond the grave, we abide in the confidence that it already has and already does. Psalm 90:2 proclaims that God's love is from everlasting to everlasting. In Christ Jesus, Christians are invited into relationship with that eternity that the psalmist describes. So even when our own laments find no pause, we remember that salvation has already been assured. We need not hear an immediate answer to prayer, because the ultimate answer to our prayers, our questions and our condition has already been given in Jesus Christ. The even better news for the doubter is that the gift has been given whether or not you believe it at this moment.

Questions for Study and Reflection

1. Read Psalm 13. How does the psalmist questions God and then proclaim faith in God. In what ways might this be a model for our own prayers?

2. Read Psalm 88. How would you write these same feelings in a modern context?

3. Think of a time you felt God drawing near. How would you describe the feeling?

4. How do we understand God to be just and loving when it appears that the wicked prosper and evil is often unrestrained?

5. How do you feel about the prayer Clarence prayed for Lynn in Ted Wardlaw's story?

6. Have you experienced prayer being answered? Was the answer what you hoped for? Have you experienced times when prayer seemed to be unanswered? How do you deal with issues of doubt and faith when that happens?

7 DEATH AND RESURRECTION

"For he has been raised." Matthew 28: 6

Death is the final question of faith in this temporal plane. It terrifies us. We fight against it for ourselves and our loved ones. It separates us from those we hold most dear. It works injustice on innocents left behind. Atrocities of war horrify us. Senseless violence shocks us. The fear of death subjects us to all sorts of manipulation: political; commercial; spiritual. It is the enemy and a powerful one at that. It is also an enemy that we will all inevitably face. Nothing in Scripture promises that we will escape facing our own deaths at some point.

This fact was brought home to a young seminarian by Professor George Buttrick, who commented in an off-handed way, "You know, everyone that Jesus healed, died." "Oh man," exclaimed the student in dismay, as the miraculous and wondrous accounts of Scripture were instantly dragged back into the reality of a finite life.

Let's examine what it means to be finite. In <u>The Nature and Destiny of Man</u>, Reinhold Niebuhr describes how we, as created beings, are limited by time, space and our own capabilities. However, he also makes the case that we have the capacity for self-transcendence. This means that we can imagine something outside ourselves, something better than the reality we experience in our current circumstances. This capacity allows us to be creative and to imagine architecture, inventions and new ideas. It allows us to conceive and pursue social justice, peace and reconciliation. It is this very transcendence that allows us to contemplate, question and ultimately embrace a faith in life beyond death. Absent this capacity for transcendence, it would be impossible for us finite creatures to grasp the idea of resurrection and eternal life.

Union Presbyterian Seminary Professor Emeritus John Leith taught most of the pastors gathered for our discussions. In his book, "Basic Christian Doctrine," Leith describes Christian hope in this way:

> The immortality about which Christian theologians have spoken is an immortality that comes as a gift from God and is sustained by the divine power. The resurrection is likewise the resurrection to eternal life. The resurrection of the body emphasizes the importance of the historical life that was expressed in and through the body and means that immortality is not a nullification of historical existence.

Thus, we see that our lives and how we live them are significant. In resurrection to eternal life, God affirms the meaning and importance of human life. Each of our lives is important in and of itself, not as a means of qualifying for heaven, either through good behavior (works righteousness) or through profession of faith (being born again). Our capacity to behave well enough or believe hard enough will always be insufficient. However, the good news we believe is that the grace of God is sufficient and has already been provided in Christ Jesus. Our salvation is not dependent upon our response to this fact, but rather we respond in gratitude because we have experienced the overwhelming love of God.

Rev. Tom Are, senior minister of Village Presbyterian Church in Prairie Village, Kansas tells a story of facing a friend's death.

> I watched my friend Stacy die. I was with her parents. She was just 17. Leukemia attacked not only her body, but also the heart of her entire family. The time came when we turned off the machines. We gathered around her bed and we read "The Lord is my shepherd." And "I will prepare a place for you."

And we read from Revelation, "There will be no more crying and no more death."

Stacy's daddy held her lifeless hand. When it comes to being a daddy of a 17-year-old little girl, we never know what to do. We never know what to say. Daddies are at a loss more times than not. We just know we would do anything … . We would do anything to protect them. We would do absolutely anything to protect them!

But she died while he held her hand. And with his heart spilling over with grief, he said, "Tom, I was so afraid that when this moment came I might not believe in heaven. But I do. I love her too much to let death take her away. You know I would not let her be taken from us if I could. Surely God loves her at least as much as I do. Surely God will refuse to grant death the power to pull her from God."

One of the deep privileges of being a pastor is to experience the power of the resurrection on a fairly regular basis. The experience of being with people through the dying process, their taking that next step, all becomes a testimony to the resurrection. Getting up there in the pulpit at a funeral and bearing witness to that resurrection, celebrating Easter every couple of weeks if you will, is a kind of spiritual discipline that makes doubt disappear for many of our ministers.

For the modern parishioner, death is not experienced this same way, as a frequently recurring rhythm in life. For the average person, death is experienced mostly within the family or close friends. It is most often felt as deep loss, rather than a next step. Sometimes we can make the leap, as an older relative is released from a time of suffering. But mostly it feels like loss. Even here, however, we can encounter the Triune God. In the nature of the Trinity, God the Father knows what it is to experience the loss of a child and God the Son knows what it is to suffer and die. Thus the range of human experience is enfolded into the essence of God and in the Holy Spirit we can take comfort.

Does trusting in such a living God constitute an argument for the truth of the resurrection? Perhaps not, but perhaps we should not be looking for such an argument. The resurrection is not to be understood as a metaphysical trick of reanimation. Rather it is the mystery of a sovereign God who can, will and has in Christ Jesus, taken an action of which only God is capable. God and God's love transcend mortal death. That is what Stacy's daddy proclaimed at her bedside.

The resurrection not only transcends human death, it transcends human ability and intellect. We should not try to explain it. It is an invitation to a mystery. This may be a new thought to a lot of people. So often we hear from the pulpit that we are the people of a resurrection faith. The implication seems to be that if you can't get on board, then we're not together. "But how do we <u>know</u> it is true?" we want to cry, and again we have sought the wrong answer.

This self-centered perspective brings with it serious dangers. If I believe that I have something right, that is I know it, then it becomes my responsibility to get others right and I become judgmental. Take our nation's recent and repugnant example of this attitude, the Phelps family and Westboro Baptist Church. Although the Supreme Court has ruled that our constitution gives them the right to protest at military funerals, their message in no way reflects a God of love and grace nor a Savior who sacrifices for our forgiveness, even at the cost of death. Theirs is a sick distortion of belief that puts themselves at the center of knowledge and judgment with grotesque consequences. Their twisted theology intentionally inflicts pain and suffering as they invade the personal and private space of another family's grief.

Alternatively, if in humility we can acknowledge the mystery and sovereignty of God, we can journey together. Our call is to live the truth of God's grace, given through the birth, life, death and resurrection of Christ Jesus, toward other people so that our witness in some small way is received as good news by them. Even if they can never take the step of saying "I believe that," that are glad we believe it because of the way we treat them. For the Christian, trust must always be prerequisite to understanding. Trust is the source of knowing God. Not knowing in terms of intellectual proof, but a knowing in terms of the certainty of love, something much broader, more fundamental, and yes, eternal.

Questions for Study and Reflection

In the sermon "Make it as Secure as You Can" in Chapter 11, John Rogers uses texts from Isaiah and Matthew to explore the mystery of resurrection.

1. What do you think about when you envision life after death?

2. There are other accounts of the dead being raised in the Bible. Read Mark 5:35-43, Luke 7:11-16, and John 11:38-44. How do these accounts compare to the account of Jesus' resurrection in Matthew 27:57 through 28:10?

3. Read Luke 24:13-35. Thinking about the Borg/Crossan paradigm of resurrection as parable regardless of factuality, what meaning do you find in the "Walk to Emmaus" story?

4. How does this sermon's invitation to mystery change your understanding of Christ's resurrection?

Frank Clark Spencer

8 LIVING IN COMMUNITY

"...with all humility and gentleness, with patience, bearing with one another in love..." Ephesians 4:2

Shepherds and flock. Teachers and students. Coaches and players. Doctors and patients. Wives and husbands. Parents and children. Ginger Rogers and Fred Astaire. Ren and Stimpy. So many things simply don't exist, don't make sense or are unimaginable, without their counterpart. There are no pastors without parishioners nor parishioners without pastors.

We have previously explored what it means to be in community, but as we begin to understand a faith community in greater depth, the unique roles of parishioner and pastor become critical to how the faith community functions. Our expectations and the personal context we bring with us into the pulpit or the pew will color our experience of worship, fellowship and mission. Like the marvelous eye-tricking art of MC Escher, one's point of view depends on where one stands. We all carry positive expectations and fearful misgivings about how other people in our lives will behave. For ministers, the response of the congregation is always felt professionally and personally. For members of the congregation, the minister's demeanor and actions can be affirming or disappointing.

Over the last several decades, the cultural pressure to attend church regularly has been lifted. Our Reformed tradition always acknowledges that God through the Holy Spirit gathers us into community. That said, the people who are in church on Sunday morning (or Saturday night) have made a choice and an effort to be there, with all kinds of mixed motives, but by choice nonetheless. They could be playing golf, or reading the *New York Times*, or traveling with children's sports teams, but they are there. This means that they come with expectations.

Likewise, pastors who have responded to the call to devote themselves to the ministry did so in anticipation of some response. It is simplistic and naïve to believe that ministers serve only from a sense of call with no regard to the impact they may have. I am reminded of the young seminarian who sought out a wise professor to confess that she had mixed motives in pursuing a career in the ministry. "Of course you do," he responded. "Now get on with it."

Too often, the others on whom we depend to help create the experience we are seeking fail to meet our internal yardstick. This goes both ways, pastors disappointing parishioners and congregations leaving pastors burned out and wondering why they have devoted themselves to ministry with seemingly little impact and even fewer material rewards. It is not that our ministers are despondent or that this is the cause for declining membership in mainline Protestant churches. This is simply another facet of doubt, questioning ourselves about how we are investing our time, talent and treasure.

Why is it that we get disappointed? More often than not, the failure of the other to please is not a fault within that person, but a different understanding of what could or should happen. How does this conflict of viewpoint manifest itself in the church? When the topic of the minister's role comes up with clergy who have been trained in our Reformed seminaries, the following descriptors are used:

    Teaching Elder;
    Preacher;
    Pastor:
    Guide;
    Servant.

When I ask Presbyterian elders from throughout the United States to give me four words to describe the minister's role, most include the word Leader or its equivalent like CEO. Other words that are most common include some of the ones listed above, particularly preacher and teacher. So there is congruence around roles of preacher and teacher. We will come back to that. But where does the lack of alignment on Leader come from?

I believe this is a part of the culture in which we live. Most Americans have become accustomed to the notion that the person with the microphone, in front of the crowd, telling us what is going on, is the leader. This image is reinforced at work, on television, in school, everywhere. We want to hear the minister preach and the physical set-up we have confirms our internal template of leader and followers. If anyone doubts the importance of these leadership expectations, just surf the web for Anthony Robinson or Tom Bandy. They have built careers around teaching leadership in Church communities. Listen to sermons and speeches at denominational gatherings. It is everywhere.

Ministers are often uncomfortable with the idea that they are leading the congregation. This discomfort is well-grounded sociologically and theologically. In discussing this topic one minister quipped, "Do you think more ministers struggle with too much humility, or too much ego?" Certainly, focus on any individual, rather than God and Christ, is dangerous. That said, our ministers must understand that they are the voice of the church for many members of the congregation. Our seminaries need to equip our future ministers with understanding and skills that they will need to provide broad leadership in their congregations.

Leavened with humility, our clergy must be willing to pick up that leadership mantle. Perhaps the pitfalls of self-focused leadership can be avoided through coming to view leadership as authorship and initiative rather than through the traditional societal lens of authority. It is not enough to teach and preach and provide pastoral care. Our ministers must ask themselves what they do to organize and enliven the body of Christ in the world after they have stepped out of the pulpit for the week.

But we disappoint our ministers with greater or equal frequency than they disappoint us. We are often selfish, mean-spirited and focused on what we want out of the church experience. Our consumer mentality isn't easy to check at the door. Pastors expect us to share with them or with each other when we suffer in our weakness, except we don't really want to do that. There are still cultural barriers to baring one's soul. TMI, too much information, we fear. That is natural and it is a two-way street. There is a boundary that the clergy don't want to cross in terms of putting too much personal information out to the congregation. The parishioner doesn't want the minister or anyone else to know how much of a sinner he really is and the minister stays reserved out of a sense of self-preservation. Those barriers can prevent the congregation from providing pastoral care for the minister in times of trouble or sorrow. On the other hand, the minister may want to find her pastoral care elsewhere, not wanting to cross those barriers within the congregation she is serving.

Some of the divide between the minister and the congregation can never be bridged. It is part of the equation. When a best friend starts telling you about your moral failings, we often say, "Stop preaching." Yet we want and expect the minister to do just that. We want an authoritative voice proclaiming the good news. We want, dare I say, a leader who can inspire us to be kinder, more forgiving, more loving, or more courageous. When the service starts, we want the minister to claim the role for which she was prepared and we want her to act like she knows what she is doing. We want to know the preacher well enough to understand that his message is authentic, but it is unlikely that we will choose the minister to socialize with on Friday night.

So here we are in community, parishioners and pastors absolutely dependent on the other, with different roles and different expectations. From the perspective of the pew, the pastor's role is the more difficult one to get just right. We demand a great orator, an erudite scholar, a compassionate comforter, a wise counselor, and a strong leader. When they meet those expectations, and they often do, we then tend to put our ministers on a pedestal and reinforce the gulf between us. We are quick to forget that our ministers are every bit as human as we are. They struggle with family relationships, wrestle with questions of faith, worry about making ends meet, care for aging parents and just like us, get tired, frustrated, sick or irritable.

How can we begin to align those expectations and know each other in ways that will strengthen our bond and allow us to "practice humility and gentleness, with patience, bearing with one another in love?" It is incumbent on the congregation to provide care for our pastors. Not in an overreaching way or in a way that becomes voyeuristic into the minister's private life, but in a way that reflects God's love for each of us in the community of faith. To receive comfort, however, ministers and parishioners alike must allow their humanity to show.

We need to think about new patterns. There are times when less formal interaction builds stronger community. We can use social media to stay in communication with brief notes that demonstrate our own humanity and care for each other. We can think about new symbolism, perhaps an invitation following the assurance of pardon to come place a hand in the baptismal font and remember that we are forever sealed in that sacrament. One minister offers "text time" to wrestle with the morning's Scripture reading during the Sunday school hour. None of these are magic formulae but each breaks down the gulf of formality between pulpit and pew.

Together, pastors and parishioners can build the community bond through embracing doubt. Through sharing our doubts, we share the human condition. We share the sorrow of a loved one's death and the doubt of where is God in this. We doubt that God or anyone else cares for us. For those going through such times, God will be found in the love and concern shown by others in the community of faith. Conversely, if the community fails to act, doubts are confirmed rather than dispelled.

We can share doubts in study together, admitting when we are perplexed by Scripture. In this, the role of minister as teacher and theologian in residence is essential. We may find that doubt also creeps into our mission work.

Gordon Cosby, whose work at the Church of the Savior in urban Washington, D. C. has been widely acclaimed, once commented, "I've raised $20 million that we have invested in this neighborhood and it's worse now than when we started." He was questioning whether it had all been of any use. Had any goals been accomplished? If we allow our faith to be tied to the outcome, whether in a neighborhood or at the bedside of someone with a terminal disease, we not only risk our own disappointment, but break down the sacred community as well.

There are members of our congregations who value the Christian faith only to the extent it furthers the causes in which they are interested. So much of how we organize reflects a corporate mentality, from strategic planning to measuring outcomes. Part of what underlies the apologetics that we discussed in Chapter 2 is a desire to have the broader culture understand why the Christian faith is viable, relevant or at least useful. The problem is, it is not enough for the Christian faith to be useful. It is much more important that it be true! We must proclaim to the world and each other that the grace of God is sufficient for all things. We should never back away from the mission of the Church to work for the world and challenge injustice, but if that's all we have, then we are going to end up as cynics, disappointed in ourselves and the Church. All that is necessary has been done for us in Christ Jesus and therefore we cannot evaluate our faithfulness by our own usefulness to the world. The Kingdom of God is not fully here and Christ's work is not yet finished.

The question for each of us is, "Do we act like Christ is Lord of the cosmos?" The answer is most often, "Usually not." There is discussion today in mainline protestant congregations about being a low expectation church. Some worry that we ask too little of ourselves and are losing members because it takes no real commitment to claim affiliation. Others worry that we ask too much of busy people and remind us that all who profess Christ as Lord are a part of the Church. Accurately discerning whether we demand too little or too much may be somewhat determinant of how our numbers continue shrinking or turn around and grow, but membership numbers will never define our faithfulness.

Will the Church have the courage to bear witness to the sovereignty of God or will we, out of our anxiety, hedge our bets. Will we live together in community, leading with conviction, sharing with courage, loving without restraint, or will what the world declares as acceptable hold sway? If it is the latter, we become little more than a community organization rather than a community of faith. I believe it is authentic community that today's "nones" are seeking. They have rejected the community organization model of congregations and long for spiritual connection.

Questions for Study and Reflection

1. Read Ephesians 4:1-6. What does it mean in practical terms to maintain the 'unity of the Spirit in the bond of Peace?"

2. What words would you use to describe the minister's role?

3. Think about ministers that you have known. How would you describe the range of styles they represent?

4. What are things your congregation does to address your pastors' needs as members of the community of faith?

5. How have you experienced a personal God who meets you where you are in your life?

6. How could your congregation live more as a community of faith rather than as a community organization?

Frank Clark Spencer

9 THANKS BE TO GOD

"For now we see in a mirror, dimly" 1 Corinthians 13:12

I worshipped recently in a non-denominational mega-church. There was so much positive energy in that place! Having often worshipped with congregations outside my own tradition, I was not surprised by much that happened. However, I was surprised by how the experience resonated with me as I thought about the people I encountered there.

The sanctuary can best be described as an auditorium that seats something over 1200 people. It is fitted with comfortable seats, a great sound system, large screens, theatrical lights, and television cameras to beam the services to the audience at home. At the same time, the architecture is spare and modern. Flowers adorned the stage, but there was no ornamentation that would let you know what kind of church you were visiting, or even that it was a church at all.

The same cannot be said of the people. You will know they are Christians by their love. Folks of all ages steamed in with Bibles. There were couples, singles, teenagers, older women and men. There were greeters with name badges and everyone was unfailingly welcoming and genuine. I felt immediately comfortable as several ushers helped me find the friend I was meeting for worship.

Then worship began. The music soared. Three men and six women spread across the stage, each with a cordless microphone.

They launched into what I would describe as modern gospel accompanied by a live five piece band. As Don McLean sings, "We all got up to dance," and in this case we got the chance. As we swayed and clapped, the words were displayed on the screen so that we could sing along. The singers led us in three extended songs. It was really participatory rather than performance oriented.

After this musical introit, we sat back down. We got messages about church activities courtesy of the big screen and a disembodied voice over the PA system. This is a real congregation with some mundane and some exciting announcements and a clear sense of community. That community was evident in the introduction of a visiting pastor from the audience who had grown up in the congregation and even more apparent in the soon to come sermon in which the pastor called his parishioners by name and joked with them along the way.

Next came a time to greet one another in the name of Jesus. Some churches might call this passing the Peace. I turned first to my friend and gave her a quick hug. I was sitting on the end of a row and so turning the other way encountered the usher who had helped me earlier. His arms were outstretched and we had a BIG hug while he told me how glad he was that I was with them tonight. Turning further, my eyes met three teenage boys sitting behind us. Each clearly wanted to greet me and each extended a hand and a hearty handshake. These were not sullen youth, compelled by parental authority to give up a Wednesday night. They were engaged and engaging.

Then came the offering. An associate pastor talked to us about tithing and commitment while the ushers, my new friend ever at the ready, handed out envelopes to anyone who might not have gotten one at the door. The young pastor let us know how much his economic fortunes had changed since he had changed his ways and made a consistent financial commitment to God through this ministry, complete with Malachi 3:10 "Bring the full tithe into the storehouse…..see if I will not….pour down for you an overwhelming blessing." We then held our envelopes aloft and prayed over our gifts, that they might strengthen this ministry to the glory of God. It was a communal prayer of dedication, with a little more direct participation than we normally experience in the mainline denominations.

This gift to God was followed by the prayers of the people. The senior pastor took over at this point, calling names and needs of those who had made prayer requests. On our feet again, we joined hands, not just with those beside us, but one of the teenagers reached around to take my hand. I realized at that moment that we were joined in one unbroken chain throughout the sanctuary, all three or four hundred of us. Not only did the pastor pray for many by name, most of whom needed healing of some physical ailment, but we were asked to pray out loud for the healing of all who were joined together in that circle. Being very comfortable in the knowledge that all humanity is broken and that we are all in need of healing of some sort, I joined right in. That free form prayer lasted at least three or four minutes.

This particular service was a teaching service that the senior pastor leads every Wednesday night. Rather than preaching from the stage, he walked back and forth in front of the auditorium and often a few feet up the center aisle. Bible in hand, he would ask questions and he expected answers from the whole assembly in a traditional call and response format. Preaching from Roman 3:4, he wanted to know, "Do you believe if God is proved true, that God is the final word on things?" The congregation shouted their affirmation. He moved from one piece of Scripture to another, transitioning seamlessly between the letters of Paul, the Psalms, Genesis, Exodus, and Job. Reading Psalm 91 as a promise from God for those who believe, his focus was on living a long and abundant life, free from disease and tragedy. We were assured that we didn't have to die in infirmity, but like Abraham, Isaac, Jacob and Joseph, we could live long lives and then peacefully expire at some age well beyond 80. As he spoke, key phrases from the Scriptures would appear on the screens. He would provide other scriptural references, telling the congregation to write them down for private reflection.

This minister is a powerful presence. In his 50's, his voice is conversational and yet commanding. The rhythm of his words pulls the listener along. The hour he talked seemed to move by quite quickly. The ministry he has built is also quite extraordinary. The church runs a large K-12 school, a seminary, a television ministry, and a women's shelter, just to mention a few of the activities.

Following the sermon, there was an invitation to the altar for any who wanted to commit to Christ, rededicate themselves to Him, join the congregation or wanted a partner to pray with them. We were reminded that if we didn't accept Christ, that we would be in Hell for all eternity, but that God did not want this for us. God wants us to come God through Jesus. This invitation brought two folks down to the front. They were greeted and handed off to waiting members of the congregation. The small group exited to loud applause.

The minister then asked for any first time visitors to come forward. With a glance to my friend, who returned an affirmative nod, off I went. I was joined by half a dozen others and we were all greeted personally. When the pastor reached me, he saw my host standing behind me and immediately said, "Oh, this is who you were telling me about." It is indeed a real community and not entertainment for entertainment's sake. Each of us was introduced to a host and we were escorted out as the benediction was given.

We were given a brief invitation to come back or consider joining, offered refreshments and received a CD of one of the pastor's sermons. My host offered to pray with me and then was happy to show me back out. I was never uncomfortable, recognizing the obvious sincerity of the hospitality.

From this account, members of most mainline protestant denominations will see there were elements that don't mesh with our Reformed perspective in terms of order of worship, approach to Scripture, or certain matters of theology. But as I went through the two hours, I found I didn't want to argue about theology or scriptural context. I was there to worship God and to be present as a way to honor the kindness of a friend. I was overtaken by a love and hospitality, the fruits of the Spirit. The folks in that sanctuary rejoiced in love and life abundant.

> For now we see in a mirror, dimly, but then we will see face to face. Now I know only in part; then I will know fully, even as I have been fully known. And now faith, hope and love abide, these three; and the greatest of these is love. (1 Corinthians 13:12-13)

Formal theological inquiry does matter, but this experience reinforces my understanding that it does not matter ultimately. John Calvin and Martin Luther could not agree enough to keep a single protestant tradition together. Karl Barth and Paul Tillich argued over important matters without resolution. Twenty-first century denominations grapple with seemingly irreconcilable differences that lead to schism. Individuals become angry at some decision and switch churches. Each of our own theologies is inherently flawed, for now we see in a mirror, dimly. Our incomplete perception will always cause us to doubt because we finite beings cannot grasp the infinite that is God.

But we are not a people without hope. For when we engage the world with the whole of our complex selves, when we open ourselves to the love of God reflected in those around us, when we humbly acknowledge the limits of our own intellect while facing doubt in all its forms, then faith allows us to proclaim, "Jesus is Lord. Thanks be to God."

Frank Clark Spencer

10 BETWEEN FAITH AND DOUBT

A sermon preached by John B. Rogers, Jr.
Davidson College Presbyterian Church, Davidson, North Carolina
c. 1975

Old Testament Psalm 42
New Testament Mark 9:2-8, 14-27
Text Mark 9:24

Raphael's painting, "The Transfiguration" shows, in the upper half of the canvas, the glorification of Christ before the awestruck disciples. In the lower half is a distraught father bringing his epileptic son in the dim hope that Christ may heal him. Our lives are lived between those two points – between overwhelming certainty and vague hope – between clarifying light and haunting darkness – between faith and doubt...sometimes closer to one, sometimes closer to the other.

John Calvin knew this as a theological fact of life. He ends the section in his <u>Institutes</u> on the Certainty of Faith by saying: "we cannot otherwise well comprehend the goodness of God unless we gather from it the fruit of great assurance." (III, 2:16)

But in the very next sentence Calvin comments on the struggle involved in faith: 'still someone will say: believers experience something far different: in recognizing the grace of God toward themselves they are not only tried by disquiet, which often comes upon them, but they are repeatedly shaken by gravest terrors. For so violent are the temptations that trouble their minds as not to seem quite compatible with that certainty of faith... We cannot imagine any certainty that is not tinged with doubt, or any assurance that is not assailed by some anxiety." (III, 2:17)

This has always been the testimony of honest belief – that faith itself is a struggle and has to be struggled for. Everybody doubts – skeptic and believer, pulpit and pew. We are talking here about genuine doubt. Not that cheap self-deception which shunts God aside in order to justify shabby conduct. Not the conceit which is always looking to call attention to itself by the airing of brilliant denials. Genuine doubt is the reverse side of genuine faith – the fathers fear that demonism and despair might have the last word, even as he cries out in trust: "Lord I believe..." Everyone doubts, and those who are honest admit it.

Likewise, everybody believes. The farmer believes in the fidelities of nature. The scientist believes the cosmos to be one and that there is an esprit de corps between his mind and this universe. The artist believes in beauty. The person who says "all is despair" still believes – in some ground of hope by which he recognizes the assurance of hope. Even St. Augustine discovered when he tried to be a total skeptic and doubt everything, that he could not really pull it off: he had at least to believe in the truth of his own skepticism, "I doubt," he was forced to conclude, "therefore truth is." There is the story of the atheist who, when asked if he were a Christian, replied angrily, "No, I'm an atheist, thank God!" Unable to trust God yet grateful for the sheer joy of life and of human love, Katherine Mansfield exclaimed, "Thanks to someone. But who?" Perhaps, suggests George Buttrick, all gratitude is belief – a (person) to (Person) call. When Kierkegaard was asked if he believed in God, he replied, "Why of course. What else?"

So everybody doubts: skeptic and believer, pulpit and pew; and everybody believes. One has little patience with a self-confident Christian who likes to make believe he has all the answers and who is quick to pass judgment on the skeptic. Bu there are skeptics also who are guilty of what one person called "the fundamentalism of unbelief" which always takes for granted that Christian doctrine or Biblical faith or this or that is by definition the most sterile orthodoxy that could ever be imagined. Indeed, the line between faith and doubt is so thin that we all keep falling off, now on this side, now on that.

For our own part, we live with this tension between faith and doubt. Our hard-won beliefs are always subject to challenge. The faith we thought we had established is called into question by a new insight. The trust we had built up is nullified by a betrayal. The creative past that was once supportive collapses under the weight of evil. The death of a single child threatens the meaning of all other lives. A betrayal by a friend destroys years of mutuality and trust. A wartime atrocity or a natural disaster nullifies belief in a God who cares for people. We can hardly live a single day without the possibility that doubt will threaten our faith.

How then do we cope with the tension? Like the student who said to his professor after class, "I wish I had never learned that; it does not fit my world view."? Or like the Arab peasant preparing one evening to eat a bowl of dates, who, after taking three different dates from the bowl and discovering, in the light of a candle, that each had a wormhole, blew out the candle and finished his meal? Or, like the father in the New Testament lesson, do we acknowledge that we live between faith and doubt: "Lord I believe; help my unbelief."?

That story of the healing of the epileptic boy has something to teach us about what it means to live between faith and doubt.

I.

First this: doubt may be an open door to greater certainty and stronger faith. There is a kind of doubt – a quality of the human spirit (or perhaps a summons to the human spirit from beyond itself) that serves to clear the air of half-truth and superstition and outworn assumptions, and that leads to breakthroughs to knowledge and to faith.

It was the practice in the middle ages for cities and countries to describe themselves by themes or mottos. At the zenith of her glory in business, banking, and culture, and as the westernmost port in Europe, Portugal adopted the motto, "Ne Plus Ultra" (nothing more beyond). But Columbus doubted, and found a new world. Beethoven doubted that the keyboard instruments of his day had reached mechanical perfection and wrote piano music that could only be played properly on instruments not yet built. Every scientific advance depends on the scientist doubting that the conclusions of his predecessors are final and acting on the basis of that doubt. We were once told that there were only six thousand stars, and so we believed until someone doubted. This doubt can be costly, even painful, but most of us would agree that the growth is worth the pain.

Dostoevsky, who knew this in a deeper sense than most of us, could say: "My Hosannas have been forged in the crucible of doubt." In Graham Greene's play, The Potting Shed, a family has been under the domination of an agnostic father who has tried to stifle all doubts from the lives of his wife and children. The family is spiritually destroyed until doubt begins to intrude in the form of an alleged miracle that shakes their unquestioned agnostic assurances. "You've spoilt our certainties," is the way Mrs. Callifer initially responds to the extraordinary claim her son is making. But she actually welcomes the new state of affairs: "it was all right to doubt the existence of God as your grandfather did in the time of Darwin. Doubt – that was human liberty. But my generation didn't doubt, we knew. I don't believe in this miracle – but I'm not sure any longer. We are none of us sure. When you aren't sure, you are alive…When you aren't sure, you are alive….."

So doubt may be the first step toward a richer, deeper and more mature faith. The New Testament Lesson deals with epilepsy which in the first century was reckoned demonic. The father doubted that anything could be done.

"<u>If</u> you can do anything…" he said to Jesus. This parent had suffered with his child, probably so much that he wondered at times if the whole of life is not epileptic – demonic. Doubt of this kind which rises up from the darkness of life and puts faith to the test is no stranger to the Christian believer. Faith in God is something people have never been able to take for granted. They have always believed in God against the outward appearances presented by the world. Their faith has always had to say, "Nevertheless" and "In spite of it all" – to confess with the Psalmist: "Nevertheless I am still with thee." (Psalm 73:23) That is what is meant by the assurance of faith. It does not mean the absence of doubt. It means living <u>with</u> doubt without living <u>by</u> doubt. It means living with doubt without fear or despair. One of the Protestant Christianity's most beloved hymns is "A Mighty Fortress." It is often requested at funerals as the Christian community stands together confessing its faith in the face of death, that final harbinger of doubt. "A mighty fortress is our God, a bulwark never failing; our helper He amid the flood of mortal ills prevailing." And yet the author of that hymn of triumph is Martin Luther, the classic doubter, who once wrote: "...faith falters, and in weakness, I cry, who knows whether it is true?" Martin Luther for whom, like countless others down the ages, doubt was the open door to deeper truth and finer faith.

II.

A second insight into the struggle between faith and doubt is that doubt alone will never provide stronger faith or deeper certainty. The advice to "cultivate one's doubts" may sometimes be a first word, but is never the last word. The last is surely that if the doubter would seek God, he must be willing to look where God has sought him, for the Christian claim is that God has taken the initiative rather than leaving it to us. And the gaze of every person, whether believer, doubter, or seeker, must be directed toward the place where God's initiative was historically expressed in Jesus Christ.

When this claim is resisted we understand why so many Protestant thinkers have described doubt as "rebellion" or sin. Sometimes the doubter turns his attention so much upon himself that he is unwilling to look elsewhere. He becomes, as Luther said, "curved in upon himself." From this perspective there is a sense in which doubt is a radical denial of God in the name of a radical affirmation of self against God. The great error here is the assumption that the reality of God is dependent on how the doubter happens to feel about God at the moment. If God exists, God will not cease to exist just because the doubter is temporarily unconvinced of God's existence. So at this point the doubter must be urged to transfer his gaze outward for a while instead of inward, to look more specifically in the direction of the One whom God has sent, to be willing to receive a gift rather than trying to create a faith, and to be content to take one step at a time.

So the father says to Jesus: "...If you can do anything have pity on us." But Jesus turns the "If" back on the father. "If you can! All things are possible to him who believes." The father was both believer and doubter. He lived with faith and with uncertainty, somewhere between the two. But he had to decide whether to live by his faith or by his doubts.

The fact is we live in a world of mystery. The absence of mystery is no sign that we have arrived at great knowledge by our intellectual acumen. Just the opposite! Albert Schweitzer said, "The highest knowledge is to know that we are surrounded by mystery." So much is mysterious that to say we will not believe until all doubt is removed is to reduce God to the level of human intelligence. Face it; there are unresolved and unrelieved enigmas in Christian faith. It is no formal garden with carefully arranged beds of flowers, but a wild, windblown forest with bottomless pools and unclassified fruits. There is no one road to truth; Christian faith is not a closed affair. Huxley found God in a search for truth. Kant found God in the search for duty. Mendelssohn found God in the search for melody. Keats found God in the search for beauty. Belief in God is not some neat system. Human beings believed long before they tried to argue for the existence of God.

Now, the Bible makes no virtue of doubt, but it knows there is no such thing as having all the answers. There may be much about Christian faith that we do not understand and much the doubter cannot believe; but there is even more he can understand and more he can believe. And that is where the search must begin – that is what it means to seek God where God has first sought us. A person may doubt, for example, that Jesus Christ is Lord and Savior or Son of God that He rose from the dead: but he may believe in the historicity of a man who "went about doing good" – who was numbered with the transgressors and outcasts of his day, because his concern for them that was not only spoken but lived. So the doubter may live on the strength of that belief. Then, sooner or later, he will have to ask himself whether that belief alone is strong enough. And as he recognizes the distance between Jesus' demands and his own obedience to these demands, he may begin to see the significance of forgiveness. And the claim that Jesus forgave sin may begin to take on for him a reality as compelling as that of his command that we love one another. Thus, the person of Jesus may become as compelling as his teaching; and Jesus himself becomes not only the mirror of a redeemed humanity, but the "mirror of the fatherly heart of God." (Luther)

As important as it is for mature faith to know and to understand what it believes, there is more to faith and discipleship than intellectual certainty. John Baillee, the late Scottish theologian said: "There are many things we may find it difficult to believe with the top of our minds, but which we believe in the bottom of our hearts." That is to say, if you could prove there is no God, I would probably still believe. If you could prove prayer was of no more significance than air vibrations, I would probably still pray. There is something which struggles after meaning and purpose and value that drives my intellect on. Augustine defined that something: "Thou hast made us for Thyself," he wrote, "and our hearts are restless 'til they rest in Thee." And so he confessed that faith, far from being a substitute for knowledge and understanding, is a foundation. "Believe," he said "in order that you may understand."

The real question for us, then, like the father in the story, is: Do we live by our doubts or by faith? The father faced his doubt — confessed it as the odds faith must meet; but he chose to live on his faith: "Lord I believe!" Faith has been called the way of courage. It has been described as tenacious and venturous, for a person has only to let go or to give up in order to doubt. Faith is creative: doubt could never have built Canterbury Cathedral. Faith brings healing whereas doubt leaves a person at odds with one's self and one's world. Faith is community — the knowledge of being loved — while doubt may be doubt of love and thus may not know deep bonds of friendship. Between faith and doubt, a person can still make a choice. "Lord, I believe!"

III.

What then we do with the doubt that plagues us? The father in the story flung his doubts upon God. He prayed his doubts: "Help my unbelief!" It is better to pray our doubts to God in a kind of trust than to splatter them on our neighbors. Another father told a friend: "Live on what you believe and work out your doubts on your knees." The father in the New Testament story sensed that if faith should vanish from the earth, his son would go unhealed and demonism would ride humankind. "Help my unbelief!" The man who prays thus knows that God alone can answer our doubt of him.

"Lord, I believe: help thou my unbelief." In a way that is the final prayer. Do not be ashamed of doubt, it says, but do not hesitate to believe. It may be the movement of God's life in our own which stirs up discontent within the doubter's soul, and it may be that the struggle for faith is necessary in order that faith may be adequate for the struggle with the demands of obedience. The doubter ought perhaps to ask why he or she is so concerned about the fact that he or she does not believe, if in fact there is nothing in which to believe. In one place Pascal puts on the lips of Jesus a curious assertion: "Console thyself," Jesus says to the agonized searcher, "thou wouldst not seek me if thou hadst not already found me." (Pensées)

"Lord, I believe: help thou mine unbelief…and Jesus took the boy by the hand and lifted him up and he arose." In the name of the Father and of the Son and of the Holy Spirit.

Resources on which this sermon drew for its material are:
"Faith and Doubt" – a sermon by George A. Buttrick
Robert McAfee Brown, The Spirit of Protestantism and also Is Faith Obsolete
Zahrnt, II, What Kind of God?

11 MAKE IT AS SECURE AS YOU CAN

A sermon preached by John B. Rogers, Jr.
Covenant Presbyterian Church, Charlotte, North Carolina
April 15, 2001; Easter Sunday

Old Testament Lesson: Isaiah 28: 14-22
New Testament Lesson: Matthew 27:57 – 28:10
Texts: Isaiah 28:21; Matthew 27:65

Introduction to the Old Testament Lesson

Our Old Testament lesson contains some of the profoundest and most powerful words the prophet Isaiah ever uttered. Facing the threat of foreign invasion, King Hezekiah and his minions have decided that trusting in the Lord of Hosts to protect his people is not enough security to suit them. They are looking to hedge their bets through alliances with other nations which invariably involved at least perfunctory worship of other gods (so as to show "good faith" toward their allies). Yes, even then rulers were only too glad to have the official approval of the religious authorities, who in their turn were only too happy to give it, conveniently ignoring the dangers to the integrity of faith and worship when throne and altar are too cozy with each other. Not much has changed.

Isaiah's warning contains the strong image of God's breaking in on human plotting, breaking through human devices, breaking up the clever plans, diplomatic and military, of those who regard God's name and God's promise as just one among many useful ways to tap into divine power to gain an advantage. Isaiah calls it God's "strange deed," God's "alien work." As the covenant people of God, says Isaiah, remember the one with whom you have to do. This is the Lord your God who, in fulfillment of his promise to deliver his people, once broke through the mighty Philistine army to give David a victory. They named a mountain on that site "Baal Perazim" – "the Lord of breaking through." This is the God who made the sun stand still over the valley of Gibeon in order to give your ancestors victory. Have you forgotten this?

Here read Isaiah 28: 14-22

Introduction to the New Testament Lesson

Our New Testament lesson tells of another strange, alien work of God breaking through human presuppositions and procedures. Our lesson begins late in the day of Jesus' crucifixion. His heartbroken followers realize that he is dead. Those who carried out the execution of this troublesome carpenter/rabbi want to make sure this problem is solved once and for all.

Here read Matthew 27:57 – 66

The Friday sun sets on the sealed tomb, secured further by a detail of armed guards. The night passes, the next day (the Sabbath), another night as the bored soldiers remain at their post. As dawn breaks on the first day of the week, something has happened – something strange, something alien. Listen:

Here read Matthew 28: 1-10

The Sermon

Several years ago during Holy Week I happened to watch a talk show in which host Charlie Rose was moderating a discussion on the meaning of Easter. His three guests were Ken Woodward, the Religion Editor of *Newsweek Magazine*; a prominent Methodist minister, and an Anglican Bishop. The longer I listened, the more irritated I became, because it was evident that the magazine reporter believed in the resurrection more passionately, and with more apparent theological understanding than did either the minister or the bishop. Ken Woodward grasped and understood the resurrection as a strange, alien, inexplicable event that was astonishing news. The others wanted to talk about the persistence of Jesus' spirit and influence, about the love that lived on in the community of faith. They felt some vocation there on national television to explain the resurrection… to render this thing compatible to the modern mind. Sad to say, the minister and the bishop seemed embarrassed by the resurrection as something inexplicable, as an unprecedented event, an alien work of which God, and God alone, is the subject.

I was reminded of something a minister friend said to the effect that to believe in the gospel you have to be willing to be embarrassed. After all, how could it be otherwise when the source of the gospel is a God who is wont to do a strange deed … an alien work? How could it be otherwise with this God who is wont to break through the sealed finality of death … to break in on what we have secured against any embarrassing eventuality, and just embarrass the life out of us by raising the dead?

I.

Notice that in telling about the resurrection, Matthew risks the embarrassment. He simply announces the resurrection of Jesus. He does not explain the resurrection. The resurrection is not described. Nothing is said about how it happened. Matthew simply proclaims that Christ is risen … more accurately, that Jesus has been raised … that God raised Jesus from the dead. Easter is not something we can analyze, explain, solve, prove, make sense of, get our minds around, fit into the dimensions of our reason, our understanding; our definition of how things are in this world. The resurrection is not a proposition; it is gospel … good news.

Matthew's Easter story is a composite of three traditions concerning the resurrection: 1) the proclamation of the resurrection, in this case by an angel; 2) the empty tomb tradition; and 3) the account of an appearance of the risen Christ.

II.

First, the announcement: the angel (a messenger of God) speaks to the women.

> **Do not be afraid; I know that you are looking for Jesus who was crucified. He is not here; for he has been raised, as he said.** (Matthew 28: 5-6)

This is the very earliest form of the Easter message. "The Lord is risen ... God raised Jesus from the dead." That was at the heart of the first Christian preaching, and it was as astounding a claim in the first century as it is today.

When the Apostle Paul preached the gospel in the Athenian Aeropagus to the modern mind of his own day, he got the attention of his audience right away.

> **Citizens of Athens, I see that you are very religious ... I have seen the statues and objects of your worship ... even that altar "to an unknown god." What you worship as unknown, I proclaim to you ... This God created the world, is the source of all life; he made of one all nations ... has put into human hearts a longing for himself ... He is not far from each one of us for, as some of your own poets have said, "In him we live and move and have our being" ... We are his offspring.** (cf. Acts 17: 22 ff)

So far, so good. These Athenians liked to discuss religion. Paul still had their attention. And then:

> **God now commands everyone everywhere to repent because he has fixed a day to measure/judge the world according to his own righteousness by a man of his own choosing** (Acts 17: 30-31)

They may have begun to get a little antsy with this talk of repenting and judgment, but they are still with him. And then:

> **... of this God has assured us all by raising this one from the dead.** (Acts 17: 31)

That word fell on them like a bombshell: no explanation, no description, no telling how this unprecedented thing happened. And there Paul lost them ... most of them:

> **Now when they heard of the resurrection of the dead, some scoffed; but others said, "We will hear you again about this."**
> (Acts 17: 32)

It was clear to the Athenians that Paul was talking about a quite alien thing. This was not the survival of Jesus' immortal soul – that, they would have understood. This was not the natural continuation of a divine life – divine beings, the Athenians knew from their own mythology, do not die. No, if the raising of Jesus from the dead was due to his "Nature," then his death on the cross was an empty charade and Good Friday is deprived of its significance. No, Matthew understands the resurrection as God's act. For this reason, the verb in verse 6 should be taken as a true passive: "He has been raised." Only because Jesus was as dead as any mortal can be was the resurrection an astonishing, alien embarrassing thing.

Well, maybe if I were on a television talk show I would not want to look foolish either. Maybe I would try to make the resurrection intellectually respectable, a logical development, so as not to embarrass the Christian church, the Presbyterian Church, my Covenant family. Maybe I too would want to protect the gospel against being made to look foolish ... maybe I too would want to make it as secure as I could within the controlling assumptions of the modern age.

III.

Next, the empty tomb.

> **Come, see the place where he lay. Then go quickly and tell his disciples, "He has been raised from the dead, and indeed he is going ahead of you to Galilee; there you will see him as I have told you." So they departed quickly**

from the tomb with fear and great joy, and ran to tell his disciples.

The earliest Christian preaching did not first announce that the tomb was empty and then conclude that Jesus had been raised from the dead. Just the opposite the resurrection is announced and then the empty tomb is lifted up, not as proof, but as a sign of the resurrection. And what does the empty tomb signify? Not, let us understand, the resuscitation of a corpse, but the miraculous reversal of death ... the transformation of Jesus' total being from death to new life by the power of God The empty tomb guards against spiritualizing the resurrection or interpreting it as the mere survival of Jesus' immortal soul. It points to the resurrection of the body ... the identifiable, embodied reality of Jesus Christ ... as the sign of God's victory over death. The scene is dominated by mystery: note the sense of awe, fear, excitement, joy. Notice, there is still no explanation here ... only the mystery of God's alien work in the risen Christ who goes before them now, and who awaits them/us at the edge of every tomorrow.

IV.

Finally, there is the appearance of the risen Christ. Mary Magdalene and the other Mary who have witnessed Jesus' death and burial are now witnesses to this alien occurrence that the angel announces and that the empty tomb signifies. They run from the sepulcher "with fear and great joy." Awe at the power of God does not inhibit their elation at the news that their crucified Lord has been raised from the dead.

And in their headlong flight, the risen Christ meets them with the stereotypical Greek greeting: "Chairete." Most English translations do not catch the emotion in that word. "Greetings!" is accurate, but the effect is weak, meaning to us no more than, "Hi there!" "Peace be with you!" is more like what Jesus would have said in his native Aramaic. Matthew is likely to have intended his readers to hear the deeper meaning of this word which is something like: "Rejoice!"

Again, much paper and ink have been spent trying to explain the nature of these appearances of the risen Christ: as visions, as hallucinations, as psychic phenomena. The fact of the matter, however, is that Easter is about the alien work of God whose action is not subject to, and will not submit to, the scrutiny of a panel of judges, whether they be academic experts, research scientists, or even theological big-wigs on a television talk show whose main concern is not to be embarrassed by Easter.

At risk of being frivolous, I would point you to that wonderful scene in the movie "Mary Poppins," where George Banks, the fastidious London banker, is sputtering about amid his joyful, ebullient children whose spirits and behavior have totally broken through the neat, orderly world he has gone to great lengths to make as secure and predictable as he can. In face of this very different sort of "alien work," Banks says:

> **Now see here, Mary Poppins, just what in blazes is going on; I demand an explanation.**

To which everybody's favorite nanny says:

> **Let me make one thing perfectly clear.**
> **I never explain anything.**

I cannot emphasize too strongly, my friends, that it is not the task of the Christian preacher or teacher or disciple to explain or prove or describe the resurrection such as to remove the scandal, and thereby allow us to domesticate this alien event. In a book titled **The Resurrection of Jesus: A Jewish Perspective**, Pinchas Lapide, an orthodox Jewish rabbi, finds the resurrection far less problematic than some Christians seem to. To this rabbi it is by no means inconceivable that the God of Abraham, Isaac and Jacob ... of Moses and Elijah and Isaiah raised Jesus of Nazareth from the grave! Although we Christians might assess the theological significance of the resurrection differently from the rabbi, his and our point of departure must be the same: what is this story telling us about God? The rabbi would remind us:

> **...the Lord (who) will break through as on Mount Perezim ...**
> **To do his deed – strange is his deed!**
> **And to work his work – alien is his work!** (Isaiah 28: 21)

As with the historical Jesus God linked his life physically and personally to ours, so with the risen Christ, God's ultimate purpose for us is embodied. Jesus' resurrection was no ectoplasmic appearance or oblong blur. The New Testament accounts are of encounters with an embodied Christ. "Reach out your hand," he said to Thomas, "and put it in my side …" (John 20:27). The bold physicality makes us wince. And Thomas's doubt gave way to confession: "My Lord and my God!" (John 20: 28). For Christians, tangibility is a portent of ultimate things to come: no vaporous soul aloft forever in spiritual skies; no passage of a droplet self into an eternal sea; no everlasting memory in the mind of God; no wistful solace based on our influence on generations to come.

In John Updike's **Pigeon Feathers**, a mother says to her son about life after death: "Think of it like Lincoln's goodness living on." To which the son replies: "But what if I'm not Lincoln? If that's all there is, then there's nothing out there but horror."

No, as the Apostle Paul said about the resurrection in his letter to the Corinthians:

God gives it a body … (I Corinthians 15: 30)

"But, but …" you say. Paul had the same "buts." He tells us that there are bodies, and then there are bodies. "There are both heavenly bodies and earthly bodies … so it is with the resurrection of the dead" (I Corinthians 15:40, 42). The accounts of the risen Jesus are strange indeed: a body that dines but "vanishes" (Luke 24: 30-31); one that can be touched (John 20:27) but not "held on to" (John 20:17). What else is this but a preview of the mystery of our own resurrection: "If there is a physical body, there is also a spiritual body" (I Corinthians 15:44). We know how to say what the spiritual body is not: it is not mortal, not "flesh and blood," not the same as we have on earth, not perishable. We end up with the apostolic finger pointing to the risen Christ, declaring with awe and great joy: "The Lord is risen." And in that alien work, we claim the promise of a future marked by embodiment, recognition, relationship, fullness of life.

What is Easter for? To comfort us all, and make of that "last enemy" a friend? My friends, it is the life-denying religions that think of death as a friend. Christian faith is a life-affirming faith. It is not the function of Easter to underscore our 'intimations of immortality,' or to marshal all the facts in support of them. In Biblical faith, when we are dead, we are dead all over! It is God who raises us into life again, by his own mighty act, even as he raised Jesus Christ from the dead.

> **For the Lord will break through as on Mount Perezim … to do his deed – strange is his deed! And to work his work – alien is his work!**

One cannot help wondering if Jesus were not thinking about that text from Isaiah when once after healing a man possessed by a demon he told about a strong man (the devil) guarding his palace: "When a strong man, fully armed, guards his castle, his property is safe. But when one stronger than he attacks him and overpowers him, he takes away his armor in which he trusted and divides his plunder" (Luke 11: 14-23).

Notice, Jesus did not say "if" or "suppose" or "perhaps" there comes a stronger one. "When one stronger than he attacks him …!" That was no frail hope, groping about in the dark, sniffing around for some thread of assurance that evil can be overcome. "When one stronger than he attacks him…! When God breaks through with his alien work…!"

Against the God of breaking through, my friends, no tomb, regardless of the steps we have taken to make it so, is secure. Thanks be to God.

Frank Clark Spencer

12 BUT SOME DOUBTED

A Sermon Preached by John B. Rogers, Jr.
Covenant Presbyterian Church; Charlotte, North Carolina
April 18, 2004

Morning Lesson: Matthew 28: 16-20

One of the marks of true faith is that it is never beyond the shadow of a doubt. Our beliefs are always candidates for earthquake. Our insights are questioned by new knowledge. Our trusts are shaken by each betrayal. Our confidence is conditioned by the fact of evil. True faith, like true love, is always vulnerable. Thus, it makes sense to ask after the place of doubt in the life of faith.

When Matthew tells of the last appearance of the risen Christ to his friends, he says very simply, and without any hint of judgment:

…And when they saw him they worshipped him; but some doubted. (Matthew 28:17)

As if to say, faith and doubt are two inevitable responses of humankind to the ways of God in the earth … two responses that are always possible, indeed that are always present, in the Christian community. The opposite of faith is not doubt, but cynicism. Cynicism – the refusal to trust anyone – is the ultimate negation. Doubt, to the contrary, is simply "faith's misgiving," for we could not doubt what does not exist, nor could we doubt that which we have not at least dimly experienced. Worship and doubt, therefore, faith and skepticism, may not be enemies but friends. And each has been represented within the community of faith since Jesus was raised from the dead.

I.

Look for a moment at the phenomenon of doubt. Why and to what end do people doubt? And what is the place of doubt in the life of faith?

One reason people doubt is that they care about the truth and want to grow. Doubt is the tool of personal, intellectual, and spiritual growth, and as such it has an important place in the life of faith. People doubt because they want to get closer to the truth. Only those who are afraid of the truth, or are content to remain static, hide from their doubts. People doubt because people care.

Columbus doubted that the world was flat. Hemingway doubted that the great American novel had already been written. A scientist doubts that the final conclusion has been reached. Dostoevsky, who was plagued by doubt, is said to have confessed: "My hosannas have been forged in the crucible of doubt."

So faith without doubt is as dead as science with no more questions to ask. Christian people – those of you who care deeply to have an informed and thoughtful faith hear this ... Christian people are not only free to doubt inside the church. We are called to doubt as one part of a faithful response to a God who, in Paul's words, gave us "this treasure (our faith) in earthen vessels, to show that the transcendent power belongs to God and not to us" (2 Corinthians 4: 7). For earthen vessels – our human ideas, concepts, theories about God – are always imperfect and fragile, in need of constant reshaping and reformation. People doubt because they care about the truth even more than they do about the vessels that bear the truth, and they want to grow.

II.

Another reason people doubt is that they are afraid that their faith is not true. This kind of doubt is harder to deal with, perhaps, because it is a product of our fear as well as our faith. It is something of a threat to us because it amounts to a calling into question of everything we have built our lives upon. All of us must wonder at times if our faith is really true, whether or not we have been swept along by our needs rather than by the evidence; or have projected a giant father image onto a cosmic screen, and have thus lived the vast majority of our lives in pretense.

Is there anything more than wish fulfillment in the forgiveness of sins? It is only to deal with my fear that I confess that God loves and is sovereign in this world? Is it really true that Jesus of Nazareth is the Christ of God, and that he was raised from the dead?

In my years of ministry, I have read the works of numerous biblical scholars and theologians on the resurrection – books and articles that deal with vital questions. What is the relation between the appearance stories and those of the empty tomb (on which the Apostle Paul, for example, is silent)? What sort of appearances were these, and where should they be placed on the interpreter's scale between "events of fact" and "events of faith"? Is the resurrection "ordinary history," or does it belong on the borderline of history, between the temporal and the eternal, the present and the future?

As far as the New Testament narrators are concerned, the Easter stories are at least "history-like." Between the telling of the story of the cross and the telling of the resurrection, no sudden and unsignaled change of reference and intention takes place, such that the crucifixion means what it says, as a temporal incident, while the resurrection has some other meaning, mythic or symbolic as distinct from the events actually described. In any case, the story of Jesus' resurrection – the empty tomb and the appearances of the risen Christ – raises the question of history and reality in the face of the biblical story. For if the tomb was not empty, if deceit and theft were behind the Easter faith, then chances are the whole business is a fake, a colossal trick played out on the stage of human pain and need! Interestingly enough, for those who saw Jesus after his death, it was not all that clear, apparently. In the presence of the risen Lord, some worshipped and some doubted.

When that kind of doubt knocks at faith's door, what do we do? First, we need to face the doubt openly and honestly, trying to lay hold of the best information on the subject we can get ... maybe in books, or in conversation with a minister or professor, or in a church school class with others whose questions must be somewhat similar.

Second, we remember that God is the source and origin of all truth; that truth leads us closer to God, not farther away; and that truth is not our enemy but our friend.

Third, we face our doubt knowing from the start that, in the end, we will not find conclusive proof either way. Rather, finally each one of us will be called on to make a venture of faith one way or another – a venture of faith and trust in a God who is not finally at the mercy of our arguments and proofs.

Fourth, we need to look for more than external evidence to make our decision. That is to say, we need to ask: what effect has this or that confession of faith had upon the lives of people? That Jesus was God with us, that he lived with us and for us as God in person, that he suffered and died with us and for us, that he has risen to reign over us as Lord of life and death ... has that made any difference to anyone I know? Has it set anyone free? Is that the source of strength and courage for people I know in times of tragedy and death? For faith is never validated by the facts alone, but finally by the power of the reality to which faith points to transform the lives of people.

Soren Kierkegaard once likened faith to "swimming in 70,000 fathoms," by which he meant that we cannot put our feet down and steady ourselves before starting out. Once we have begun to swim we cannot expect any assurance beyond the shadow of a doubt, as though when the going got tough the ocean floor would rise up to meet our feet. The final validation of our decision to get in the water is whether we sink or swim, whether the faith for the struggle is sufficient to help us make it in the struggle for faith.

> **...Because we look not to the things that are seen, but to the things that are unseen; for the things that are seen are transient, but the things that are unseen are eternal.** (2 Corinthians 4: 18)

And so doubt, in keeping us honest in the tension between the seen and the unseen, has an important place in the life of faith.

III.

Another reason people doubt is that sometimes they fear that their faith is not false, but true! Sometimes we doubt because we fear that faith's claims may indeed be true, and that they may revolutionize our style of life. "Why is it so hard to believe?" Pascal once asked, "Because it is so hard to obey!"

"Part of the reason I could not find God," said the great Scottish theologian John Baillie,

> **...was that there is that in God which I did not wish to find. Part of the reason I could not (or thought I could not) hear God speak was that he was saying some things to me I did not wish to hear. There was a side to God which was unwelcome to me, and some divine commandments the obligatoriness of which I was most loathe to acknowledge. And the reason I was loathe to acknowledge them was that I found them too disquieting and upsetting, involving for their proper obedience a degree of courage and self-denial ... such as I was not altogether prepared to face.**

There was another side to God that I did want, Baillie went on to say in so many words, and I was disturbed when I could not get it. Some things about God I yearned to hear, to know, and to have, and when I could not, I began to doubt God altogether.

> **But because there were other of his words to which I turned a deaf ear, my deafness seemed to extend even to that for which I was most eagerly listening.**

The point is: sometimes we create our own image of God, then look for God and, when we cannot find the God we created, we doubt that God exists at all. Said Augustine to God in his <u>Confessions</u>:

He is thy best servant who looks not so much to hear from thee what conforms to his own will, as rather to conform his will to whatsoever he hears from thee.

For we cannot turn a deaf ear to what God requires of us without also becoming deaf to what God promises us. Or, as Baillie puts is:

We cannot be assured of God's care if we reject God's claim.

So again doubt is a kind of tribute that honesty pays to faith. Sigmund Freud was right when he told us that our beliefs are determined more than we know by our desires. So honest doubt keeps us from finding the gods we make, and keeps us open to being found of the God who made us. Thus it has an important place in the life of faith.

IV.

At least one further reason people doubt is because there seems to be a conflict between what faith claims and how life routinely works out. Faith claims that God is both powerful and loving. But, if God is powerful, it is sometimes hard to believe in his love, for so much happens in this world that real love could not allow. And, if God is loving, then it is hard to trust God's power, for love is so easily defeated.

The Christian faith ought not to treat such doubt lightly, or claim that the issue is resolved. It does give us Christ as our clue, however, that God is in this business of life with us, sharing whatever it is we have to bear, wrestling with it along with us, seeking as we seek to bring some good out of even the worst that we must face. But, when all is said and done, there is no proof that this is so. True faith is always vulnerable, never beyond the shadow of a doubt. Therefore, if our doubts keep us insecure, open, questing ... if they make us finally unwilling to settle for shallow, immature, self-serving and simplistic answers ... if in the midst of all else that is finally untrustworthy our doubts teach us to trust in the trustworthiness of God, and in God alone ... then doubt has an important place in the life of faith.

V.

But the Bible never treats doubt as a virtue, for people cannot long live on their doubts any more than they can be nourished by food they refuse to eat. To keep on saying, "Is it true?" is like endlessly saying, "Is this food?" Unless one eats, one is likely to starve. Doubt has a creative place in the life of faith only for so long; then each person must make his or her own venture. Author John Updike makes his venture:

> **I call myself a Christian by defining a Christian as a person willing to profess the Apostles' Creed. I am willing, unlike most of my friends – many more moral than myself – to profess it (which does not mean understand it, or fill its every syllable with the breath of sainthood), because I know of no other combination of words that gives such life, that so seeks the crux. The Creed asks us to believe not in Satan, but only in the hell into which Christ descends. That hell, in the sense at least of a profound and desolating absence, exists, I do not doubt; the newspapers give us its daily bulletins. And my sense of things, sentimental I fear, is that wherever a church spire is raised, though dismal slums surround it and a single dazed widow kneels under it, this hell is opposed by a rumor of good news, by an irrational confirmation of the grace we feel is our birthright.**

Let me try to put that in images appropriate to our lives here and now:

- Wherever a church spire is raised…
- Wherever a group of men, women, and young people gather briefly in the middle of a busy, demanding day of commerce and toil and trade to worship God…
- Wherever the word of God is proclaimed and the sacrament celebrated with integrity…

- Wherever the reality of God's grace and command presses upon the consciousness of a community…
- Wherever the ethos of a culture or a city includes the weight and presence of a Life beyond our own from whom and through whom and to whom are all things…
- Wherever the compassion of God in Christ takes shape in the ministries of a church in the urban heart of a city …

There hell – the power of evil, sin, and death – is opposed by more than a rumor of good news. There hell is met by an unyielding God consciousness, by a persistent Christ-perspective, by a dogged faith-dimension within human hearts and in our life together.

One of the things that helps me in my venture is the realization that there is a difference between belief and trust. If I hear a lecture on the physical universe in which the lecturer assumes that there is mind behind matter, then I can say, "That person believes in God." But if I could follow the lecturer home and listen in as he prays: "O Lord, watch over my family; give me wisdom and courage and direction in what I think and say and do; and keep me close to your heart," then I know something else much deeper about his faith. I know to whom he trusts his life. Faith in a proposition about the existence of God is belief. But faith in a God who can be addressed in adoration, in confession, in gratitude, in intercession, in person … that is trust. Our beliefs in propositions are basic to us, and without them we could not live. But in the final analysis, we live not by our beliefs but by whom we trust. In fact, many people have been held fast by their trust in the trustworthiness of God while in periods of doubt they have struggled with their various beliefs. For, at its heart, the gospel is not a series of propositions to be believed. It is the good news that there is someone we can trust, someone who had us in mind before we were born, called us into existence for a purpose, loves us with a love that simply will not let us go, and who wants us for his sons and daughters.

So the problem of faith and doubt is never settled by argument. Someone once said: "It is often easier to act yourself into a new way of thinking than to think yourself into a new way of acting." The acid test of any faith is its capacity to be lived on with integrity. We resolve our doubts on the way, on the Pilgrim way. We test our beliefs in the living of them. And we trust in God's gift of faith for the struggle to sustain us in our struggle for faith.

Which is surely why not just the worshipers, but the "some" who doubted continued and were included in that company who received Christ's final claim, his final command, and his final promise:

> **And when they saw him they worshipped him; but some doubted. And Jesus said to them: "All authority has been given to me in heaven and on earth. Go therefore and make disciples of all nations, baptizing them in the name of the Father, and of the Son, and of the Holy Spirit, teaching them to observe all that I have commanded you. And lo,...**

(This promise to you who are honest enough to doubt even as you worship, and you who have courage and trust enough to worship even though you doubt:)

> **...Lo, I am with you always, to the close of the age.**

In the name of the Father, and of the Son, and of the Holy Spirit. Amen.

Frank Clark Spencer

BIBLIOGRAPHY

Basic Christian Doctrine, John Leith, Westminster John Knox Press, 1993

Being Wrong: Adventures in the Margin of Error, Kathryn Schulz, Harper Collins, 2010

The Book of Confessions, Presbyterian Church (USA), 2007

The Book of Order, Presbyterian Church (USA), 2007

Church Dogmatics, A Selection, Karl Barth, T&T Clark, 1961

Dynamics of Faith, Paul Tillich, Harper and row, 1957

Evangelical Theology, Karl Barth, Self-published 1963

The Institutes of the Christian Religion, Volumes 1&2, John Calvin, Westminster John Knox Press, 2006

The Language of God, Francis Collins, Free Press 2006

The Lord of the Rings, JRR Tolkien, 1954, United States printing Ballantine Books, 1965

Mere Christianity, C. S. Lewis, C.S. Lewis Pte. Ltd., 1980, United States printing Harper Collins, 2001

The Nature and Destiny of Man, Reinhold Niebuhr, Charles Scribner and Sons, 1941, Westminster John Knox Press, 1996

Frank Clark Spencer

ABOUT THE AUTHORS

Frank Clark Spencer is the President of Habitat for Humanity Charlotte and a student in the Masters of Divinity program at Union Presbyterian Seminary. Before turning to full-time ministry, Frank had an outstanding business career which included creating one of North Carolina's 50 largest public companies, leading the company to its initial public offering on the New York Stock Exchange, and being recognized by Ernst and Young as 2009 Entrepreneur of the Year for the Carolinas. Frank has been an Elder in the Presbyterian Church (USA) since 1994, is the past Chairman of Montreat Conference Center and currently serves on the Presbyterian Board of Pensions. He was a Morehead Scholar at the University of North Carolina Chapel Hill and was named a Baker Scholar at Harvard Business School. You may find additional information at www.FSpencer.com.

John B. Rogers, Jr is a Presbyterian minister. He completed his B.D. and Th.M. degrees at Union Theological Seminary in Richmond, VA, and was ordained in July of 1967. He taught in the Department of Religion and was college chaplain at Presbyterian College in Clinton, SC. His pastorates include First Presbyterian Church, Durham, NC (Associate Pastor), Davidson College Presbyterian Church, First Presbyterian Church, Shreveport, LA., and Covenant Presbyterian Church in Charlotte, NC. He has served on the Board of Trustees of Austin Presbyterian Theological Seminary, Union Theological Seminary in Virginia, and Davidson College and now lives in Montreat, NC, where he continues to preach occasionally and to teach at local churches, conferences and retreats as well as at Union Presbyterian Seminary in Charlotte.

Made in the USA
Lexington, KY
23 February 2014